TASTE OF SUMMER

ISBN 1 74022 572 4 EAN 9 781740 225 724 © Robyn Martin © Photographs: Concept Publishing Limited unless credited below.

Originally published by Concept Publishing Limited. This edition published by R&R Publications Marketing Pty. Ltd. 12 Edward Street, Brunswick 3056.
Victoria, Australia. Phone: 03) 9381 2199 Fax: 03) 9381 2689 Australia wide toll-free: 1800 063 296.

E-mail: info@randrpublications.com.au. Web: www.randrpublications.com.au No part of this publication may be produced in any form or by any means electronic or
mechanical, including photocopying, recording, or any information storage and retrieval system, without the permission in writing from the publisher.

Printed in China by Kings Time Printing.

TASTE OF SUMMER

Robyn Martin

R&R PUBLICATIONS MARKETING PTY LTD

CONTENTS

INTRODUCTION

Summer is special season. It really is the one we all live for, work towards and make our biggest plans around.

For us, summer means drying out and warming our bones after an inevitably cold, miserable winter. It means having a holiday, working in the garden, painting the house, relaxing at the beach and taking time to plan for the new year.

Summer provides opportunities for different approaches to food. Our meals are full of fresh fare – vegetables, fruit and freshly caught fish. We approach meals and entertaining with casual enthusiasm but it doesn't take long to tire of the ubiquitous barbecued sausage and bowl of strawberries.

Summer is a great time and the recipes that follow provide summer food choices that take us beyond the blackened sausage and strawberry bowl to new angles on old favourites more suited to the lifestyle we now enjoy.

Robyn Martin

FRESCO
NACKS

ining over summer is one of the special

or a more relaxed approach to enjoying the

nds and family.

now who is going to pop in, so it pays to keep

gredients on hand to transform into a snack to

ss of wine or a cup of coffee.

TASTE OF SUMMER

MARINATED MUSHROOMS

These can be served as a salad if wished but they make a delicious addition to an antipasto platter.

100g button mushrooms

1 small clove garlic

2 tablespoons extra virgin olive oil

2 tablespoons lemon juice

1/4 teaspoon marjoram leaves

Freshly ground black pepper

If mushrooms are very small, leave whole. If not, slice thinly. Crush and peel garlic and cut into slivers. Mix the mushrooms, olive oil, lemon juice, marjoram, garlic and freshly ground black pepper together. Leave to marinate for at least 2 hours or overnight. Serve as part of an antipasto platter.

Serves 6.

PESTO

This is one recipe where you need to use fresh basil to achieve a successful result.

3/4 cup tightly packed fresh basil leaves

1 clove garlic

Pinch salt

1/4 cup olive oil

1/4 cup toasted pinenuts

25g grated parmesan cheese

Place basil in the bowl of a food processor or mortar. Crush and peel the garlic. Add to basil with the salt and half the oil. Process, or pound with a pestle, to a smooth pate. Add pinenuts and remaining oil and process or pound until the nuts are lightly chopped. Add the parmesan cheese and process to mix in. Use as wished. To store pesto, pour into a container, smooth surface and pour over extra olive oil. Cover and refrigerate for up to a week or freeze into small blocks or in ice cube tray.

Makes about 3/4 cup.

TASTE OF SUMMER

TOMATO SALSA

Use brown onions if red are unavailable. Red onions have a milder flavour better suited to uncooked dishes.

4 tomatoes

1 red onion

¼ teaspoon Mexican chilli powder

¼ cup chopped fresh coriander or parsley

1 tablespoon lemon juice

Salt

Freshly ground black pepper

   Cut tomatoes in half and remove seeds. Use these in another dish. Cut flesh into small cubes, about 5mm. Peel and finely chop onion. Mix tomatoes, onion, chilli powder, coriander or parsley and lemon juice together. Season with salt and freshly ground black pepper. Use to fill pita bread, or serve as a meat accompaniment.

Makes about 2 cups.

HUMMUS

Use this as a dip or as a thick sauce to spread in a pita bread pocket before adding sliced barbecued meat and salad. It's delicious. Tahini is a sesame seed paste and is available in the health or ethnic food section of the supermarket.

310g can chick peas or 1 cup cooked chick peas

3 tablespoons tahini

¼ cup lemon juice

1 clove garlic

¼ cup oil

   Drain chick peas. Place chick peas, tahini and lemon juice in the bowl of a food processor or a blender. Crush and peel garlic. Add to chick peas. Process until chick peas are chopped. Gradually add oil down the feed tube and process until mixture is smooth and the required consistency for use.

Makes about 1 cup.

Tomato Salsa in Pita Pockets & Hummus.

TASTE OF SUMMER

MARINATED OLIVES

1 clove garlic

¹/₂ cup pitted black olives

¹/₂ cup extra virgin olive oil

1 teaspoon rosemary

Freshly ground black pepper

Crush and peel the garlic. Place olives in a bowl. Add oil, rosemary and garlic. Grind black pepper over olives and set aside for flavours to develop.

Makes ¹/₂ cup.

MELON WITH PROSCIUTTO

This sounds very off shore but really it's not. Prosciutto is a raw ham cured by a long salting process. It is readily available but if you can't obtain it try this idea using smoked beef or pork kassler.

4 small slices honeydew or rock melon

8 thin slices prosciutto

Cut the rind from the melon leaving a well shaped wedge of melon. Wrap two slices of prosciutto around the melon to cover the centre area of the melon.

Serves 4.

CROSTINI WITH PESTO

12 1¹/₂cm thick slices french bread

Extra virgin olive oil

¹/₄ cup pesto

Brush both sides of bread with olive oil and toast at 190°C for 2 to 3 minutes or until golden. Spread with pesto. Return to oven for 1 minute. Serve warm or cold.

Makes 12.

Marinated Olives (right), Melon with Prosciutto (left), Crostini with Pesto

TASTE OF SUMMER

13

VOL AU VENTS WITH HAM AND ASPARAGUS

If fresh asparagus is unavailable, drain a can of asparagus and chop into 2cm lengths. Mix into the sauce.

12 fresh asparagus spears

1 x 1cm thick ham steak

1 small onion

25g butter

2 tablespoons flour

1¼ cups milk

Salt

Pepper

1 teaspoon prepared french mustard

575g packet vol au vents

Break ends off asparagus and discard. Cut spears into 5cm lengths from the tip. Place asparagus spears and trimmed ends in a frying pan of boiling water. Boil for 3 minutes. Turn off heat and stand in pan for 5 minutes. Drain. Cut trimmed ends into small pieces. Trim rind from ham steak. Cut flesh into ½cm cubes. Peel onion and finely chop. Melt butter and saute onion for 5 minutes or until clear. Remove from heat and stir in flour. Return to heat and cook until frothy. Remove from heat and stir in milk. Cook, stirring until mixture boils and thickens. Stir in salt, pepper, mustard, ham and asparagus ends. Cook vol au vent cases according to packet directions. Fill cases with ham and asparagus filling. Cut each asparagus tip in half lengthwise and place in each filled case. Reheat at 180°C for 5 to 10 minutes or until hot.

Makes 24.

SMOKED SALMON AND SOUR CREAM VOL AU VENTS

575g packet vol au vents

250g pot low fat sour cream

1 tablespoon wholeseed mustard

1 tablespoon chopped fresh dill

2 tablespoons finely chopped walnuts

100g packet smoked salmon

Dill

Cook vol au vent cases according to packet directions. When lightly golden, remove from oven and lift out pastry round in top of vol au vents. Leave to cool. Mix sour cream, mustard, dill and walnuts together. Half fill each vol au vent case with the sour cream mixture. Cut each slice of smoked salmon into three. Arrange in vol au vent case. Top with a little more sour cream mixture. Garnish with dill. Serve at room temperature.

Makes 24.

Vol au Vents with Ham and Asparagus and Smoked Salmon and Sour Cream Vol au Vents

MUSHROOM BONBONS

These make an interesting entree served with a fresh sauce. To stop the pastry ends collapsing, place something ovenproof in to hold them up. Our solution was a glass ball normally used for flower arrangements. Make sure you count how many you use and account for them all before you serve these.

200g mushrooms
2 cloves garlic
1 medium onion
2 tablespoons oil
2 tablespoons chopped parsley
³/₄ cup low fat sour cream
400g packet flaky puff pastry
1 egg
16 chives

Wipe mushrooms, trim and slice thinly. Crush, peel and chop garlic. Peel onion and chop finely. Heat oil in a frying pan and saute onion, garlic and mushrooms over a high heat for 3 to 4 minutes. Drain if necessary. Add parsley. Cool, then mix in sour cream. Roll pastry out on a lightly floured board to 2mm thickness. Cut into 15 x 10cm rectangles. Place one tablespoon of mushroom mixture down the centre of each pastry rectangle to within 3cm of either end. Wet one edge of pastry. Roll pastry around filling, sealing wet edge against pastry. Bunch ends up to form a bonbon shape. Lightly beat egg and brush bonbons with this. Place on a baking tray. Bake at 200°C for 10 to 15 minutes or until golden and cooked. Tie chives around each end of cooked bonbons before serving.

Makes 8.

Mushroom Bonbons and Blue Cheese, Pear and Walnut Triangles

BLUE CHEESE, PEAR AND WALNUT TRIANGLES

100g wedge blue vein cheese

¹/₂ cup roasted walnuts

2 canned, drained pear quarters

4 sheets flaky puff pastry

EGG WASH

1 egg

1 tablespoon water

Crumble blue cheese into a bowl. Finely chop walnuts. Cut pears into small pieces. Mix cheese, walnuts and pears together. Cut pastry into 8cm squares. Place one teaspoon of filling onto one half of pastry. Brush pastry edges with egg wash. Fold pastry in half to form a triangle, pressing the edges together. Cut a small hole in the top. Brush top with egg wash. Bake at 200°C for 10 minutes or until pastry is golden.

EGG WASH

Combine egg and water together.

Makes about 36.

FILO FLAKES WITH SPINACH SCRAMBLE

These cases can be made ahead of time and stored in an airtight container.

4 sheets filo pastry

Melted butter

SPINACH SCRAMBLE

1 small onion

1 tablespoon oil

¼ cup finely chopped, well drained, cooked spinach

3 eggs

2 tablespoons milk

Pinch nutmeg

Salt

Freshly ground black pepper

Cut pastry sheets into thirds. Brush each third with melted butter. Place one piece into greased deep mini muffin tins. Top with a second piece, then a third piece, turning the pastry around each time so the pastry points don't line up. Bake at 200°C for 10 minutes or until lightly golden. Remove from pans and cool on a cooling rack. Fill with spinach scramble. Serve warm.

SPINACH SCRAMBLE

Peel onion and finely chop. Heat oil in a frying pan and saute onion for 5 minutes until clear. Add spinach. Lightly beat eggs and milk together. Pour into pan with onion and spinach and cook over a medium heat until starting to set. Pull a wooden spatula through the mixture to break into clots. When set, season with nutmeg, salt and pepper. Use to fill filo flakes.

Makes 18.

CURRIED SWEET POTATO TURNOVERS

2 medium sweet potatoes

2 spring onions

1 teaspoon curry powder

½ cup low-fat sour cream

400g packet crusty pie pastry

Poppy seeds

Peel sweet potatoes and cook in boiling salted water until tender. Drain and cool. Trim spring onions and slice thinly. Cut sweet potatoes into 1cm cubes. Mix with spring onions, curry powder and sour cream. Roll pastry out on a lightly floured board to 2mm thickness. Cut into twelve squares. Place one tablespoon of sweet potato mixture on the middle of one half of each pastry square. Wet edges. Press edges together to form an envelope. Lightly press poppy seeds onto each turnover. Place on a baking tray. Bake at 190°C for 15 minutes or until golden. Serve warm.

Makes 12.

CAMEMBERT AND HAM FLATS

3 sheets flaky puff pastry

3 tablespoons pesto

2 slices ham off the bone

100g round camembert

Fresh basil leaves

Cut pastry into 4 x 11cm rectangles. Spread each rectangle with pesto. Chop ham finely. Sprinkle ham over pesto. Bake at 190°C for 10 to 15 minutes or until cooked. Cut camembert into ½cm slices. Place two pieces of camembert over each pastry rectangle. Serve garnished with fresh basil leaves.

Makes 24.

Camembert and Ham Flats, Curried Sweet Potato Turnovers and Filo Flakes with Spinach Scramble

ASPARAGUS WITH PASTRAMI AND STRAWBERRIES

12 asparagus spears

8 slices pastrami or prosciutto

12 small strawberries

12 small satay sticks

Break ends off asparagus. Trim spears to even lengths. Place asparagus in a frying pan of boiling water. Simmer for 5 minutes. Turn heat off and stand for a further 5 minutes. Drain and refresh under cold water. Roll pastrami into small tight rolls. Cut into three. Hull strawberries. Thread asparagus, pastrami roll, strawberry, pastrami roll and the remainder of the asparagus spear onto a small satay stick.

Makes 12.

OTHER IDEAS

• Use drained canned asparagus and thread with hardboiled quail eggs.

• Use corned beef and potato cubes from a readymade potato salad instead of the pastrami and strawberries.

Asparagus with Pastrami and Strawberries

SUSHI

3 nori sheets

3 cups cooked short grain rice

2 tablespoons white vinegar

1 tablespoon sugar

$^1/_4$ teaspoon salt

1 egg

3 tablespoons pickled ginger

$^1/_2$ x 185g can tuna

Place nori sheets on a clean tea-towel. Combine rice, vinegar, sugar and salt together. Divide rice mixture among the nori sheets, spreading out to within 2cm of the edge. Whisk egg and pour into a small non-stick frying pan. Cook to form a small omelet. Cut in 2cm long strips. Place three strips in the middle of the rice with 1 tablespoon of pickled ginger and one-third of the tuna. Using a tea-towel as an aid, roll nori and filling up to form a tight cylinder. Cut into 2cm wide slices. Serve with wasabi and extra pickled ginger.

Makes 30.

OTHER IDEAS

- Replace tuna, egg and pickled ginger with cooked chicken strips, thin strips of blanched carrot and strips of canned or fresh mango.

- Replace tuna, egg and pickled ginger with sliced smoked salmon and mashed avocado or drained canned asparagus.

Sushi

21

THAI STYLE PRAWNS

2 tablespoons sweet chilli sauce

2 tablespoons soy sauce

30 medium-sized prawns

15 small satay sticks

2 tablespoons chopped fresh coriander

Mix chilli and soy sauces together. Toss prawns in sauce mixture. Thread two prawns onto each skewer. Grill for 2 to 3 minutes on a barbecue hot plate or in the oven until hot and golden. Serve sprinkled with chopped fresh coriander.

Serves 4 to 6.

Thai Style Prawns

CURRIED PEANUT CHICKEN NIBBLES

125g packet salted peanuts

1 teaspoon curry powder

¹/₂ cup toasted breadcrumbs

2 eggs

2 tablespoons cornflour

18 chicken nibbles

3 tablespoons oil

Place peanuts in a food processor and finely chop. Alternatively finely chop with a knife.

Mix peanuts, curry powder and breadcrumbs together. Lightly beat eggs and cornflour together. Dip chicken nibbles in egg mixture then in the crumb mixture. Heat oil in a roasting dish. Place chicken nibbles in the dish. Turn to coat in oil. Bake at 180°C for 20 minutes or until cooked. Serve warm or cold.

Makes 18.

Note: Chicken nibbles are made by cutting several chicken tenderloins into bite size pieces.

fully delicious

Curried Peanut Chicken Nibbles

SMOKED CHICKEN WITH MINTED MELON

Sometimes the most simple ideas work the best. This is so easy but so delicious and refreshing too.

1 smoked chicken
1 honey dew melon
Mint leaves
15 to 20 medium-size satay sticks

Remove skin from chicken. Cut into 2cm cubes. Peel melon and roll flesh into balls. Thread a melon ball, mint leaf and smoked chicken cube onto a satay stick.

Makes 15 to 20.

OTHER SKEWERED IDEAS

- Wrap small pieces of melon with prosciutto and serve on a toothpick.

- Skewer marinated button mushrooms and stoned olives.

- Brush wedges of avocado with lemon juice. Thread one end onto a skewer then thread a small roll of cooked bacon, then the other end of the avocado.

Smoked Chicken with Minted Melon

SOUND OF MUSIC ROLLS

4 sheets mountain bread
PASTRAMI AND PESTO FILLING
2 tablespoons pesto
4 slices pastrami
ASPARAGUS, HAM AND EGG FILLING
280g can asparagus
6 slices ham
3 hard-boiled eggs
2 tablespoons mayonnaise
Salt
Pepper

PASTRAMI AND PESTO FILLING

Spread two sheets of mountain bread with pesto. Arrange pastrami on top. Roll up like a sponge roll. Cut into 3cm wide rolls.

ASPARAGUS, HAM AND EGG FILLING

Drain asparagus and mash. Chop ham finely. Mix asparagus and ham together and spread over two sheets of mountain bread. Shell and chop eggs finely. Mix with mayonnaise, salt and pepper. Spread over the asparagus mixture. Roll up like a sponge roll. Cut into 3cm wide rolls. Arrange on a serving platter.

Sound of Music Rolls

TASTE OF SUMMER

TASTE OF SUMMER

SAVOURY BREAD CASES

10 slices bread
Butter or olive oil spray
FILLING
1 small onion
2 teaspoons oil
310g can cream style corn
2 slices ham
1 tablespoon chopped parsley

Spread bread with butter or spray with olive oil. Remove crusts. Cut bread into rounds and use to line patty tins, buttered side down. Bake at 190°C for 10 minutes until crisp and lightly golden. Fill with hot filling and serve.

FILLING

Peel and finely chop onion. Heat oil in a frying pan and saute onion for 5 minutes or until clear. Mix onion with corn. Chop ham and add to corn with parsley. Heat filling until boiling. Use to fill the bread cases.

Makes 10.

OTHER FILLING IDEAS

- Smoked fish in parsley sauce.

- Curried egg mayonnaise.

- Cream cheese, chopped ham and drained crushed pineapple.

- Guacamole topped with tomato salsa.

- Cooked chopped bacon and scrambled eggs.

KNIGHTS ON HORSEBACK

1 tablespoon capers

$^1/_2$ cup cream cheese

18 pitted prunes

6 rashers bacon

Drain capers. Chop finely. Mix with cream cheese. Use to fill the stone cavity of the prunes. Derind bacon. Cut each rasher into three pieces. Wrap a bacon piece around a prune. Secure with a toothpick. Bake at 180°C for 3 to 5 minutes.

Makes 18.

CORN CHIPS WITH BITS

450g can refried beans

1 teaspoon Tabasco sauce

200g packet tortilla chips

2 cups grated tasty cheese

Mix beans and Tabasco sauce together. Place a teaspoon of mixture on each tortilla chip. Sprinkle over cheese. Cook under a hot grill for 1 to 2 minutes until cheese is melted and golden.

Savoury Bread Cases (top), Knights on Horseback and Corn Chips with Bits

CHEATS' LAVASH BREAD

2 sheets Naan bread

2 tablespoons olive oil

2 teaspoons lemon pepper

2 tablespoons finely chopped red pepper

1 teaspoon paprika

Place Naan bread on a board and brush with olive oil. Cut into 8 x 8cm squares and transfer to a baking tray. Sprinkle evenly with lemon pepper, chopped red pepper and paprika. Bake at 180°C for 5 to 10 minutes or until golden brown.

Serves 4 to 6.

HOT AND SPICY CHEESE STRAWS

1 cup flour

1 teaspoon baking powder

1/4 teaspoon salt

50g butter

1/2 cup grated tasty cheese

2 teaspoons Tabasco sauce

2 eggs

3 tablespoons water

2 tablespoons sesame seeds

EGG WASH

1 egg

2 tablespoons water

Combine flour, baking powder and salt together. Rub butter into flour to form fine breadcrumbs. Add cheese and Tabasco sauce. Beat eggs and water together and add to flour mixture. Knead mixture together to form a firm dough. Chill for 20 minutes. Roll dough out on a floured board to form a 25 x 20cm rectangle. Cut into 1cm long strips and then knot the ends. Place on a greased baking tray and brush tops with the egg wash. Sprinkle over sesame seeds. Bake at 180°C for 10 minutes or until golden. Cool.

EGG WASH

Combine egg and water.

Makes 20.

Cheats' Lavash Bread and Hot and Spicy Cheese Straws

SUMMER BARBECUES

There was a time when the barbecue was a three-legged charcoal barbie in the backyard and much time and talk was spent preparing our summer speciality – chargrilled sausages. They were the ones you couldn't tell apart from the charcoal if they had the misfortune to fall into the fire.

Now the gas barbie has hit town and there is a whole new look and taste for the backyard barbecue. Smart sausages, hamburgers, stir fries, Mexican fare and succulent steaks now fill our plastic plates.

It's a relief when summer comes. The barbecue is cleaned off and the taste of summer cooking begins.

TASTE OF SUMMER

From bottom left: Chicken in Thai Marinade,
Lamb in Satay Marinade & Beef in Simple Chilli Marinade.

SATAY MARINADE

2 cloves garlic

1 small onion

2 tablespoons lemon juice

1 tablespoon peanut oil

¼ cup peanut butter

2 tablespoons soy sauce

1 tablespoon brown sugar

1 tablespoon grated root ginger

½ teaspoon chilli powder

Crush, peel and mash garlic. Peel onion and finely chop. Mix garlic, onion, lemon juice, oil, peanut butter, soy sauce, brown sugar, ginger and chilli powder together in a bowl or plastic bag. Add food to be marinated and turn to coat. Cover or seal and marinate for 2 hours at room temperature or overnight in the refrigerator. Remove from marinade and cook on the barbecue.

Makes enough marinade for 375g beef, lamb, pork or chicken.

THAI MARINADE

½ cup coconut milk

2 teaspoons grated lemon or lime rind

2 tablespoons lemon or lime juice

2 tablespoons chopped fresh basil

1 tablespoon chopped fresh coriander

¼ cup sweet chilli sauce

Mix coconut milk, grated rind, juice, basil, coriander and chilli sauce together in a bowl or plastic bag. Add the food to be marinated and turn to coat. Cover or seal and marinate for 1 hour at room temperature or overnight in the refrigerator. Remove from marinade and cook on the barbecue.

Makes enough marinade for 500g beef, lamb, pork or chicken.

SIMPLE CHILLI MARINADE

1 clove garlic

¼ cup soy sauce

2 tablespoons sweet chilli sauce

Crush and peel garlic. Mix garlic, soy sauce and chilli sauce together in a bowl or plastic bag. Add the food to be marinated and turn to coat. Cover or seal and marinate for 1 hour at room temperature or overnight in the refrigerator. Remove from marinade and cook on the barbecue.

Makes enough marinade for 250g beef, lamb, pork or chicken.

TASTE OF SUMMER

GINGER MARINADE

1 clove garlic

1 tablespoon sesame oil

2 tablespoons soy sauce

1 tablespoon grated root ginger

1 tablespoon honey

Crush and peel garlic. Mix garlic, sesame oil, soy sauce, ginger and honey together in a bowl or plastic bag. Add the food to be marinated and turn to coat. Cover or seal and marinate for 1 hour at room temperature or overnight in the refrigerator. Remove from marinade and cook on the barbecue.

Makes enough marinade for 250g beef, lamb, pork, chicken or fish.

CHINESE MARINADE

2 cloves garlic

2 tablespoons honey

4x2mm slices root ginger

¼ cup soy sauce

Crush and peel garlic. Warm honey. Mix garlic, ginger, honey and soy sauce together in a bowl or plastic bag. Add the food to be marinated and turn to coat. Cover or seal and marinate for 1 to 2 hours at room temperature or overnight in the refrigerator. Remove from marinade and cook on the barbecue.

Makes enough marinade for 250g beef, lamb, pork, chicken or fish.

Fish in Ginger Marinade, Beef in Szechuan Marinade, Lamb in Spicy Malaysian Marinade & Pork in Chinese Marinade.

SPICY MALAYSIAN MARINADE

2 cloves garlic

2 fresh red chillies

2 tablespoons grated root ginger

¼ cup lime juice

1 teaspoon grated lime rind

¼ cup red wine vinegar

2 tablespoons finely chopped coriander

½ teaspoon sugar

Crush and peel garlic. Deseed and finely chop chillies. Mix garlic, chillies, ginger, lime juice, lime rind, vinegar, coriander and sugar together in a bowl or plastic bag. Add the food to be marinated and turn to coat. Cover or seal and marinate for 2 hours at room temperature or overnight in the refrigerator. Remove from marinade and cook on the barbecue.

Makes enough marinade for 500g beef, lamb, pork, chicken or fish.

SZECHUAN MARINADE

2 cloves garlic

¼ cup soy sauce

½ cup plum sauce

2 teaspoons grated lemon rind

¼ cup lemon juice

1 tablespoon sesame oil

1 tablespoon grated root ginger

½ teaspoon chilli powder

½ teaspoon Chinese five spice powder

½ teaspoon ground coriander

Crush, peel and mash garlic. Mix garlic, soy and plum sauces, lemon rind, lemon juice, sesame oil, ginger, chilli and five spice powders and coriander together in a bowl or plastic bag. Add the food to be marinated and turn to coat. Cover or seal and marinate for 2 hours at room temperature or overnight in the refrigerator. Remove from marinade and cook on the barbecue.

Makes enough marinade for 375g beef, lamb, pork or chicken.

WENDY'S RUB

1 large clove garlic

1 tablespoon prepared wholeseed mustard

1 tablespoon cracked black peppercorns

Oil

½ cup chopped parsley

Crush, peel and mash garlic. Mix garlic, mustard and peppercorns together. Brush beef, lamb, pork or chicken with oil. Spread garlic mixture over then roll in parsley. Cook on the barbecue grill.

MOROCCAN RUB

1 onion

2 cloves garlic

½ teaspoon ground cinnamon

½ teaspoon ground ginger

1 teaspoon ground cumin

¼ teaspoon turmeric

¼ teaspoon chilli powder

¼ cup olive oil

Peel and finely chop onion. Crush, peel and finely chop garlic. Mix onion, garlic, cinnamon, ginger, cumin, turmeric and chilli powder together. Add oil and mix well. Press the mixture over beef, lamb or chicken. Stand at room temperature for about 1 hour then cook in a covered barbecue until meat or poultry is cooked. If a covered barbecue is unavailable wrap meat or poultry in foil and cook on the barbecue grill. Makes enough to cover 1 leg of lamb, 1 whole beef fillet or 1 large chicken.

Whole Fillet with Wendy's Rub & Chicken in Moroccan Rub.

TASTE OF SUMMER

SAUSAGES WITH MUSTARD AND BACON

500g precooked sausages

About 1 tablespoon prepared American mustard

6 rashers bacon

Toothpicks

Spread sausages with mustard. Derind bacon and wrap around the sausages in a spiral fashion. Secure with toothpicks. Cook on the barbecue grill until bacon is golden and sausages heated through.

Serves 4.

HAMBURGER PATTIES

1 onion

500g lean mince

¾ cup soft breadcrumbs

1 tablespoon Worcestershire sauce

1 tablespoon tomato or chilli sauce

1 teaspoon beef stock powder

2 tablespoons chopped parsley

Freshly ground black pepper

Peel and finely chop onion. Mix onion, mince, breadcrumbs, sauces, stock powder, parsley and freshly ground black pepper together. With wet hands, divide into 6 patties. Flatten slightly and grill on the barbecue until cooked through. Serve in toasted hamburger buns with salad, mustard, pickles and tomato sauce.

Makes 6.

Sausages with Mustard & Bacon & Hamburgers.

SPICY ORANGE MARINADE

1 small onion

½ cup orange juice concentrate

2 tablespoons vinegar

2 bay leaves

½ teaspoon ground allspice

Peel onion and finely chop. Mix onion, orange juice concentrate, vinegar, bay leaves and allspice together in a bowl or plastic bag. Add food to be marinated and turn to coat. Cover or seal and marinate for 2 hours at room temperature or overnight in the refrigerator. Remove from marinade and cook on the barbecue.

Makes enough marinade for 250g beef, lamb, pork or chicken.

BEER MARINADE

1 clove garlic

½ cup tomato sauce

1 cup beer

2 tablespoons Worcestershire sauce

2 tablespoons brown sugar

1 tablespoon prepared wholeseed mustard

1 tablespoon cornflour

Crush and peel garlic. Mix garlic, tomato sauce, beer, Worcestershire sauce, brown sugar, mustard and cornflour together in a bowl or plastic bag. Add the food to be marinated and turn to coat. Cover or seal and marinate for 2 hours at room temperature or overnight in the refrigerator. Remove from marinade and cook on the barbecue.

Makes enough marinade for 500g beef, lamb, pork or chicken.

Pork in Spicy Orange Marinade & Beef in Beer Marinade.

TASTE OF SUMMER

MINCED MEAT KOFTAS

These are really like meatballs, so don't be put off by a different sounding name.

1 onion
2 cloves garlic
500g lean beef or lamb mince
1 tablespoon chopped fresh mint
1 teaspoon salt
2 teaspoons ground cumin
¼ teaspoon ground allspice
1 egg
Oil
Satay sticks or metal skewers

Peel onion and grate. Squeeze out onion juice and discard. Crush, peel and finely chop garlic. Place mince in a bowl and mix in onion, garlic, mint, salt, cumin, allspice and egg. Mix until well combined. With wet hands, shape into 4–5cm long cylinders. Thread onto soaked satay sticks or metal skewers. Brush with oil and cook on the barbecue grill or hotplate, turning frequently until cooked through. The outside should be crisp. Serve in pita bread with raita and tomato salsa.

Serves 4 to 6.

BEEF SATAY

500g rump steak
2 teaspoons turmeric
2 teaspoons ground cumin
½ teaspoon grated lemon rind
1 teaspoon salt
¼ cup coconut milk
About 12 satay sticks

Cut meat into 15mm cubes. Mix turmeric, cumin, lemon rind, salt and coconut milk together. Add meat and stir to coat. Marinate meat in coconut mixture for 2 hours at room temperature or overnight in the refrigerator. Soak satay sticks in warm water for 30 minutes. Thread meat onto the sticks and cook on the barbecue grill until the required doneness. Serve with satay sauce.

Serves 4.

SEAFOOD FRITTERS

1 cup chopped fresh marinated mussels, or whitebait, or strips of firm white fleshed fish

1 cup flour

¾ teaspoon baking powder

¼ teaspoon salt

1 egg

¾ cup milk

Oil

Lemon wedges

Drain fish if necessary. Sift flour, baking powder and salt into a bowl. Add egg and sufficient milk to make a smooth batter. Stir fish into batter. Lightly oil barbecue hotplate. Use about ¼ cup of batter to make each fritter. Pour onto the hotplate and cook over a moderate heat until golden. Turn and cook the other side. Serve hot with lemon wedges.

Serves 6.

SATAYS

500g chicken breast fillets

or 500g pork fillets

or 500g beef fillets

Marinade

Satay sticks

Cut chicken, pork or beef into thin strips lengthwise. Marinate in any marinade of your choice. Thread onto soaked satay sticks, weaving the stick down the length of the chicken, pork or beef strips. Preheat barbecue to a medium heat and cook satays for 5 to 6 minutes, turning frequently until cooked.
Serves 4.

Minced Meat Koftas, Raita & Tomato Salsa in Pita Pockets, Seafood Fritters & Chicken & Beef Satays.

MIXED GRILL SKEWERS

2 cloves garlic

8 lamb middle loin chops

Lemon pepper

Oil

8 rashers bacon

8 chipolatas

4 sheep kidneys

8 button mushrooms

8 bay leaves

Metal skewers

Crush, peel and mash garlic. Rub chops with garlic. Sprinkle with lemon pepper. Oil long metal skewers. Derind and cut bacon rashers in half. Roll up like a sponge roll. Thread a bacon roll onto each skewer. Bend chipolatas in half and thread onto skewers. Thread another bacon roll onto skewer so it pushes tightly against the chipolatas. Halve kidneys removing the core. Thread chops onto skewers then a piece of kidney, a mushroom and a bay leaf. Grill on the barbecue until the required doneness.

Serves 8.

Mixed Grill Skewers (left), Chicken Tandoori & Mexican Steak Fajitas.

TASTE OF SUMMER

MEXICAN STEAK FAJITAS

This is a good dish to serve when you have a lot of people to feed.

750g piece rump steak

2 cloves garlic

¾ cup orange juice

1 tablespoon oil

2 tablespoons red wine vinegar

2 tablespoons lemon juice

Pinch cayenne pepper

¼ teaspoon ground cumin

Freshly ground black pepper

Tortillas

Trim any fat from meat. Crush, peel and mash garlic. Mix garlic, orange juice, oil, vinegar, lemon juice, cayenne pepper and cumin together in a bowl or plastic bag. Add meat and turn to coat. Cover or seal and marinate overnight in the refrigerator. Remove from marinade and grill over a hot barbecue until brown on the outside but still pink inside. To serve, cut meat thinly across the grain. Serve with freshly ground black pepper and serve on warm tortillas with fried onions, guacamole and tomato salsa.

Serves 6.

CHICKEN TANDOORI

This recipe works very well in a covered barbecue, or on a motorised rotisserie, but can be barbecued directly on the barbecue cookware as well.

1 large chicken

2 cloves garlic

200g pot natural unsweetened yoghurt

1 tablespoon grated fresh ginger

2 teaspoons turmeric

1 teaspoon paprika

2 teaspoons garam masala

1 teaspoon ground cardamom

¼ teaspoon chilli powder

Cut chicken in half through the back and open out so as the chicken lies flat. Crush, peel and mash garlic. Mix garlic, yoghurt, ginger, turmeric, paprika, garam masala, cardamom and chilli powder together. Brush chicken all over with this mixture. Cook over a hot barbecue grill for about 45 minutes, turning halfway through cooking or until the chicken is cooked. Brush chicken with any left-over yoghurt mixture during cooking. To serve, cut into portions.

Serves 4 to 6.

SUMMER SALADS

Coleslaw has been, and probably always will be, a part of barbecue entertaining, but after a few barbecues and functions you can be forgiven if you tire of this salad mainstay.

The bounty of fresh vegetables available in the warm summer months provides so many opportunities for exciting salad combinations.

Use these recipes as a guide and make your own salad combinations with whatever you have available.

It's often the dressing that gives a salad the 'x' factor and the pages that follow provide plenty of exciting x-rated choices.

YOGHURT DRESSING

If you are counting calories or watching your fat intake, try this as a low-fat, low-energy alternative to mayonnaise.

1 cup natural unsweetened yoghurt
2 tablespoons wine vinegar
1 tablespoon lemon juice
1/4 teaspoon salt
Freshly ground black pepper

Mix yoghurt, vinegar, lemon juice, salt and pepper together until combined.

Makes 1 1/4 cups.

SWEET CHILLI DRESSING

Try this with rice or pasta salads or stir fry mixtures for an oriental flavour.

1/2 cup sweet chilli sauce
3 tablespoons sesame oil
1 tablespoon soy sauce
2 tablespoons malt vinegar
1 teaspoon very finely chopped root ginger

Mix chilli sauce, sesame oil, soy sauce, vinegar and ginger together until combined.

Makes about 3/4 cup.

From bottom left: Blue Cheese Dressing, Sweet Chilli Dressing, Tahini Dressing and Yoghurt Dressing

BLUE CHEESE DRESSING

Blue cheese and pears are a delicious combination. This dressing goes with many salads but try serving it with poached pears and walnuts as a simple entree.

100g blue vein cheese
3/4 cup soya bean oil
2 tablespoons wine vinegar
Freshly ground black pepper

Place the cheese, oil, vinegar and pepper in the bowl of a food processor or blender and process until smooth and creamy.

Makes 1/4 cup.

TAHINI DRESSING

This is delicious with chick peas and lentils, or for a nutty taste in salads. Tahini is sesame seed paste and can be bought in the herb and spice or international section of the supermarket.

1 clove garlic
1/4 cup tahini
1/4 cup lemon juice
1/4 teaspoon ground cumin
1/2 cup olive oil

Crush and peel garlic. Place garlic, tahini, lemon juice and cumin in the bowl of a food processor or blender. With the motor running, slowly pour the oil down the feed tube, processing until combined.

Makes 1 cup.

QUICK HOME-MADE MAYONNAISE

Different oils will give this mayonnaise different flavours. Use a light olive oil if you aren't heavily into the flavour of virgin olive oil.

2 egg yolks
1/2 teaspoon salt
1 teaspoon prepared mustard
2 tablespoons white vinegar
2 tablespoons lemon juice
1 1/2 cups olive oil

Place the egg yolks, salt, mustard, vinegar and lemon juice in the bowl of a food processor or blender. Process to combine. With the motor running, slowly pour the oil down the feed tube in a thin, steady stream. Process or blend until thick and creamy.

Makes about 1 1/2 cups.

ALISON'S GREEN DRESSING

This is one of the more versatile dressings to have in your repertoire. I use it as a dip with toasted pita bread, as a sandwich spread or just as a dressing, or serve it with steamed fish. It is superb.

1 clove garlic
2 eggs
1/4 cup white vinegar
1 teaspoon salt
1/2 teaspoon sugar
1 teaspoon prepared mustard
1/4 cup roughly chopped mixed herbs such as chives, parsley and dill
1 1/2 cups soya bean oil

Crush and peel garlic. Place eggs, vinegar, salt, sugar, mustard, garlic and herbs in the bowl of a food processor or blender. Process or blend until garlic is chopped and ingredients combined. With the motor running, slowly pour the oil in a very thin, steady stream down the feed tube. Process until creamy.

Makes about 2 cups.

AIOLI

5 cloves garlic

1 egg

1 tablespoon lemon juice

1 teaspoon prepared french mustard

½ teaspoon salt

Freshly ground black pepper

¾ cup light olive oil

Crush and peel garlic. Place garlic, egg, lemon juice, mustard, salt and pepper in the bowl of a food processor or blender. Process until garlic is finely chopped and ingredients combined. With the motor running, slowly pour the olive oil down the feed tube of the food processor in a thin, steady stream until a mayonnaise consistency forms.

Makes about 1 cup.

GREEN PEPPERCORN MAYONNAISE

Try this with a steak or smoked fish or just a salad.

2 tablespoons green peppercorns in brine

1 cup mayonnaise

1 teaspoon whole grain mustard

Wash and drain peppercorns and crush lightly with the back of a knife or in a mortar and pestle. Mix mayonnaise, peppercorns and mustard together.

Makes 1 cup.

ROASTED RED CAPSICUM MAYONNAISE

Serve this in any recipe using mayonnaise for a different flavour. For a change, try it in a potato salad or with fish.

1 red capsicum

1 cup mayonnaise

4 drops Tabasco sauce

Cut capsicum in half. Remove the seeds and grill until the skin blisters. Remove from oven and wrap in a paper towel. When cool, remove skin. Puree capsicum flesh in a food processor or blender. Mix capsicum puree, mayonnaise and Tabasco sauce together.

Makes 1¼ cups.

TABBOULEH

Having a few basic herbs in your garden always provides extra flavour in a salad. You need plenty of fresh parsely and mint for this favourite.

1 cup cracked wheat
Boiling water
4 spring onions
3 tomatoes
1 onion
1 cup finely chopped parsley
½ cup chopped mint
¼ cup lemon juice
¼ cup olive oil
Large pinch chilli powder
Salt

Place wheat in a bowl and cover with boiling water. Leave to soak for 15 minutes. Drain and wash under cold water. Drain well and dry on a tea towel or paper towels. Place wheat in a bowl. Finely slice spring onions. Cut tomato into cubes. Peel and finely chop onion. Mix spring onions, tomatoes, onion, parsley, mint, lemon juice, oil and chilli powder into wheat. Season to taste with salt.

Serves 6.

MINT AND ALMOND TABBOULEH

1 cup cracked wheat / boiling water
3 spring onions
¼ cup chopped parsley
2 tablespoons chopped mint
2 hard-boiled eggs
¼ cup toasted slivered almonds
¼ cup olive oil
¼ cup lemon juice
Salt and pepper
2 tablespoons chopped chives

Pour boiling water over the wheat. Leave until the water is cold, then drain well. Trim the spring onions and slice finely. Mix wheat, spring onions, parsley and mint together. Shell the eggs and chop finely or mouli if wished. Add to the wheat with the almonds. Mix oil and lemon juice together. Pour over the salad and toss to mix thoroughly. Season to taste with salt and pepper. Garnish with chopped chives. Serve with pita bread.

Serves 4 to 5.

TASTE OF SUMMER

From top left clockwise: Tabbouleh, Tim's Stir Fry Rice Salad, Rice and Sesame Salad and Mint and Almond Tabbouleh

TIM'S STIR FRY RICE SALAD

This is for my son, Tim, who discovered Chinese food wasn't poisonous when he learnt to stir fry chicken and rice. It's a great way to use left-over rice. The Sweet Chilli Dressing recipe is on page 47.

3 tablespoons peanut oil

3 cups cold cooked rice

4 rashers bacon

3 spring onions

2 eggs

1 tablespoon sherry

¼ to ½ cup Sweet Chilli Dressing

Heat the oil in a wok or large frying pan. Stir fry the rice until lightly browned. Remove from heat and place in a bowl. Leave to cool. Derind the bacon and cut flesh into 1cm strips. Stir fry bacon in the wok until cooked. Add to rice. Trim spring onions and cut into 2cm pieces on the diagonal. Add to rice. Lightly beat eggs and sherry together. Pour half into the hot wok and turn wok to make a thin omelet. Cook until set. Roll omelet up and cut into ½ cm strips. Add to rice. Repeat with remaining egg. Pour over Sweet Chilli Dressing and toss to coat. Serve at room temperature.

Serves 4.

RICE AND SESAME SALAD

1 cup quick-cooking brown rice

8 button mushrooms

3 spring onions

¼ cup roasted cashew nuts

¼ cup white vinegar

1 tablespoon soy sauce

1 tablespoon sesame oil

½ teaspoon sugar

Cook rice according to directions on the packet. Drain well and cool. Wipe mushrooms and slice thinly. Trim spring onions and cut into 1cm slices on the diagonal. Mix rice, mushrooms, spring onions and cashews together in a bowl. Mix vinegar, soy sauce, sesame oil and sugar together. Pour over rice mixture and toss to combine.

Serves 4.

POTATO SALAD VINAIGRETTE

6 medium potatoes

1 red onion

2 rashers bacon

¹/₄ cup chopped parsley

¹/₂ cup vinaigrette

Peel potatoes. Cut into wedges or chips and cook in boiling salted water until just tender. Drain well and place in a bowl. Peel the onion and cut into rings. Mix with the potatoes. Derind and cook the bacon. Drain on a paper towel and cut into 1cm pieces. Mix the bacon, parsley and vinaigrette through the potatoes.

Serves 6.

CURRIED POTATO AND EGG SALAD

The amount of curry powder for this recipe will depend on your taste and the type of curry mix you use.

6 medium potatoes

4 hard-boiled eggs

¹/₄ cup chopped chives

2 sticks celery

¹/₂ cup mayonnaise

2 to 3 teaspoons curry powder

1 tablespoon finely chopped coriander

Peel potatoes. Cut into cubes and cook in boiling salted water until just tender. Drain well and place in a bowl. Shell the eggs and chop roughly. Add to the potatoes with the chives. Wash and trim celery. Cut into thin slices. Add to the potatoes. Mix the mayonnaise and curry powder together and carefully mix through the potato mixture, taking care not to break up the potatoes. Garnish with chopped coriander.

Serves 4 to 5.

From bottom left clockwise: Curried Potato and Egg Salad; Potato Salad Vinaigrette; Spinach, Orange and Bacon Salad and Greek Artichoke Salad

SPINACH, ORANGE AND BACON SALAD

250g spinach

2 oranges

2 rashers bacon

2 spring onions

2 tablespoons white vinegar

1 tablespoon orange juice

¼ cup oil

1 teaspoon dried tarragon

Salt

Freshly ground black pepper

Wash spinach and remove stalks. Break leaves into small pieces. Peel oranges with a small sharp knife, removing the pith. Cut the orange segments between the membranes and add to the spinach. Derind the bacon and cook until crisp. Trim the spring onions and cut into 1cm pieces, slicing on the diagonal. Crumble the bacon over the spinach and add the spring onions. Mix the vinegar, orange juice, oil, tarragon, salt and pepper together in a screw-top jar. Shake to combine. Pour over the spinach mixture and toss to combine. Serve immediately.

Serves 6.

GREEK ARTICHOKE SALAD

400g can artichoke hearts

440g can carrots

3 spring onions

2 tablespoons white vinegar

1 tablespoon orange juice

¼ cup oil

2 tablespoons wine vinegar

2 tablespoons fresh dill

Freshly ground black pepper

Drain the artichoke hearts and carrots. Wash and trim the spring onions. Cut into thin slices on the diagonal. Scrub the potatoes and cook in boiling water for about 10 minutes or until tender. Drain well. If using canned potatoes, drain well. Shake the oil, vinegar, dill and freshly ground black pepper together in a screw-top jar. Mix the artichoke hearts, carrots, spring onions and potatoes together. Pour over the dressing and toss to coat.

Serves 4.

Al's Cauliflower Salad

My sister, Alison, is another salad expert. This is one of her favourites.

1 small cauliflower
2 bananas
2 tablespoons lemon juice
1¹/₂ cups fresh or drained canned peach slices
¹/₄ cup toasted almonds
¹/₂ cup natural unsweetened yoghurt
¹/₂ cup mayonnaise
Snow pea sprouts

Trim and wash the cauliflower. Place whole in a saucepan of boiling water and cook for 5 minutes. Alternatively steam or microwave. Drain well and cut into florets. Leave to cool. Peel bananas. Slice into 2cm pieces on the diagonal. Toss in lemon juice. Mix the cauliflower, bananas, peaches and almonds together in a bowl. Combine the yoghurt and mayonnaise. Carefully mix through the cauliflower mixture. Garnish with snow pea sprouts.

Serves 6.

Sweet and Sour Broccoli Salad

500g broccoli
440g can pineapple rings in juice
1 ham steak
¹/₄ cup reserved pineapple juice
2 tablespoons sesame oil
1 tablespoon white vinegar
1 tablespoon toasted sesame seeds

Wash and trim the broccoli. Cut into florets. Cook in boiling salted water for 5 minutes. Drain and refresh under cold water. Drain. Leave to cool. Drain the pineapple, reserving ¹/₄ cup of juice. Cut pineapple rings in half. Trim rind from ham steak and cut flesh into strips or cubes. Mix broccoli, ham and pineapple together. Mix reserved pineapple juice, sesame oil and vinegar together in a screw-top jar. Pour over broccoli mixture and toss to coat. Garnish with toasted sesame seeds.

Serves 4 to 5.

Spring Asparagus and Strawberry Salad

500g fresh asparagus
2 spring onions
2 shallots
2 cups strawberries
2 tablespoons cider vinegar
2 tablespoons oil
Freshly ground black pepper

Break tough ends from asparagus then cut spears into even pieces about 3cm long. Cook in boiling water for 5 minutes. Drain well and refresh in cold water. Drain. Place in a serving bowl. Trim spring onions and cut into 1cm pieces, slicing on the diagonal. Peel shallots and slice thinly. Separate rings. Hull the strawberries. Reserve half a cup of strawberries. Leave remaining strawberries whole if small, otherwise cut in half. Add spring onions, shallots and strawberries to asparagus. Puree reserved strawberries in a food processor or blender. Add vinegar and oil and blend well. Pour over asparagus mixture or serve separately. Garnish with freshly ground black pepper.

Serves 3 to 4.

Al's Cauliflower Salad, Sweet and Sour Broccoli Salad and Spring Asparagus and Strawberry Salad

INSALATA ABRUZZO

If you aren't an anchovy fan, leave these out. This is a delicious salad, with or without anchovies.

250g green beans

2 onions

80g can anchovies

4 tomatoes

2 red or yellow capsicums, or one of each

3 zucchini

¹/₂ cup basil leaves

¹/₄ cup wine vinegar

¹/₂ cup olive oil

Pinch chilli powder

Top and tail the beans. Cut in half and cook in boiling water for 10 minutes, or until just tender. Drain and refresh in cold water. Drain. Peel onions and slice thinly. Drain anchovies and cut into 2cm pieces. Deseed tomatoes and cut flesh into ¹/₂ cm slices. Deseed the capsicums and cut into thin strips. Trim ends from zucchini. Cook whole in boiling water for 4 minutes. Drain and cut into thick slices. Cut basil leaves into thin strips. Mix beans, onions, anchovies, tomatoes, capsicums, zucchini and basil together. Shake vinegar, oil and chilli powder together in a screw-top jar. Pour over vegetables and toss to coat.

Serves 6 to 8.

PANZANELLA

Now don't turn your nose up at this for a salad idea. Keep an open mind. Try it – it's delicious. It does need specialty bread. Just any old stale bread won't do.

6 slices stale Italian or French bread

4 spring onions

1 cucumber

4 tomatoes

½ cup basil leaves

½ cup vinaigrette

Soak the bread in cold water for 5 minutes. Squeeze out as much water as possible and refrigerate while preparing the remaining ingredients. Trim spring onions and slice finely. Slice the cucumber thinly and cut tomatoes into cubes. Cut basil leaves into thin strips. Mix spring onions, cucumber, tomatoes, and basil together. Place half of mixture in a serving bowl. Layer bread over this and top with remaining cucumber mixture. Pour over vinaigrette and toss lightly.

Serves 4 to 5.

TROUVILLE TOMATO SALAD

This is a simple and delicious way to serve tomatoes.

4 medium tomatoes

1 clove garlic

1 tablespoon chopped parsley

1 tablespoon vinaigrette

Slice the ends off the tomatoes and discard. Cut tomatoes into 2mm-thick slices. Crush and peel the garlic. Rub garlic all over the inside of the bowl or platter to be used for serving. Discard the garlic. Arrange the tomato slices in the bowl or on the platter. Sprinkle with chopped parsley and drizzle with vinaigrette.

Serves 4.

From top left clockwise:
Trouville Tomato Salad,
Panzanella and
Insalata Abruzzo

TASTE OF SUMMER

Avocado and Lime Salad

If limes aren't available use lemons and don't be put off by the chilli powder. Mexican chilli powder is a mild chilli, giving flavour without too much heat.

1 clove garlic	
2 ripe avocados	
4 tomatoes	
3 limes	
1 green capsicum	
$1/4$ cup lime juice	
$1/2$ teaspoon Mexican chilli powder	

Crush and peel garlic. Rub garlic all over the inside of the serving bowl to be used. Peel and destone the avocados. Cut flesh into $1^1/2$ cm cubes. Blanch tomatoes in boiling water for 1 minute. Drain and refresh tomatoes in cold water. Peel skin from tomatoes. Cut tomatoes, remove seeds and cut flesh into 1cm cubes. Using a small sharp knife, peel skin and pith from limes. Cut segments between membranes. Squeeze and reserve any juice from lime membranes. Cut capsicum in half. Deseed and cut flesh into 1cm cubes. Mix avocado, tomato, lime, capsicum, lime juice and chilli powder together, folding carefully so avocado does not break up. Leave for 2 hours for flavours to develop.
Serves 5 to 6.

Greek Salad

6 medium tomatoes	
250g feta cheese	
1 cup black olives	
$1/2$ cup basil leaves	
3 tablespoons olive oil	
Freshly ground black pepper	

Cut stem end from tomatoes and discard. Slice tomatoes thickly and arrange on a serving platter. Crumble feta over tomatoes and arrange olives over. Break basil leaves into pieces and scatter over the tomatoes. Drizzle oil over tomatoes and coarsely grind over black pepper.
Serves 4.

CAPSICUM AND MUSHROOM SALAD

250g button mushrooms

1 small red capsicum

1 small green capsicum

4 spring onions

12 black olives

DRESSING

2 tablespoons spiced vinegar

2 teaspoons sugar

1 small clove garlic

1 teaspoon chopped fresh tarragon or

½ teaspoon dried tarragon

1 tablespoon chopped chives or garlic chives

1 teaspoon wholegrain mustard

¼ cup low-fat sour cream

Wipe the mushrooms and cut into quarters. Deseed and thinly slice the red and green capsicums. Slice the spring onions. Arrange mushrooms, capsicums, spring onions and olives in a serving bowl. Pour dressing over and toss. Serve immediately.

DRESSING

Heat vinegar and sugar together until sugar dissolves. Remove from heat. Crush, peel and mash the garlic. Add to the vinegar mixture. Stir in the tarragon, chives, mustard and sour cream.

Serves 6.

*Avocado and Lime Salad (top),
Capsicum and Mushroom Salad
and Greek Salad*

CAESAR SALAD

This salad makes my mouth water at the thought of it. Serve it as a light luncheon meal or as a vegetable accompaniment. The name has nothing to do with Roman times but was first made in Tijuana, Mexico, at Caesar's Palace, by Italian immigrant Caesar Cordini. It soon crossed the Mexican border and became an American classic.

4 cloves garlic
1/4 cup olive oil
3 cups french bread cubes
1 to 2 cos lettuce
1/2 teaspoon salt
3 tablespoons lemon juice
1/4 cup olive oil
1/2 teaspoon Worcestershire sauce
3 lightly hard-boiled eggs
1/2 cup grated or shaved parmesan cheese
8 anchovy fillets

Crush and peel the garlic. Mash two cloves of garlic and mix with first measure of olive oil. Mix well so garlic flavours oil. Brush oil over bread cubes. Place bread on baking tray and bake at 180°C for 10 to 15 minutes or until golden, turning occasionally, to make croutons. Wash and dry lettuce. Tear leaves into pieces and place in a bowl. Mash remaining garlic with salt. Mix garlic, lemon juice, second measure of olive oil and Worcestershire sauce together. Pour over lettuce. Shell eggs and chop roughly. Sprinkle over parmesan cheese and toss to mix. Cut anchovies into pieces and place on top of salad with croutons.

Note: For lightly hard-boiled eggs, cook for 5 minutes.

Serves 4 to 6.

From back left clockwise: Caesar Salad, Corn Salad with Avocado Dressing and Waldorf Salad.

CORN SALAD WITH AVOCADO DRESSING

2 cups frozen whole kernel corn
1 red capsicum
1 green capsicum
3 spring onions
2 sticks celery
1 ripe avocado
1/2 cup lemon juice
1/4 cup sour cream
1 teaspoon Mexican chilli powder

Cook the corn in boiling water for 2 minutes. Drain well and refresh in cold water. Drain. Deseed capsicums and cut into 1cm cubes. Trim spring onions and celery and slice thinly. Mix corn, capsicums, spring onions and celery together. Peel and destone avocado. Mash with a fork until smooth. Mix the avocado, lemon juice, sour cream and chilli powder together. Mix avocado dressing through corn mixture or serve separately.

Serves 4 to 6.

WALDORF SALAD

The original recipe for this American salad is nearly 100 years old. It was first made by Oscar Tschisky at the Waldorf Astoria Hotel at the end of the 19th century. The original Waldorf Salad was minus the walnuts. These were added around 1928. It is best made with home-made mayonnaise.

4 red-skinned apples
2 tablespoons lemon juice
3 sticks celery
1/2 cup walnut quarters
3/4 cup mayonnaise

Cut apples into quarters. Core and cut into slices or cubes. Place in a bowl and mix with lemon juice. Trim celery and cut in 1cm slices. Mix apples, celery and walnuts together and fold through mayonnaise. If wished serve garnished with extra walnuts.

Serves 6 to 8.

TASTE OF SUMMER

SPINACH AND EGG SALAD

DRESSING

2 cloves garlic
1 teaspoon English mustard
Freshly ground black pepper
$^1/_4$ cup spiced vinegar
1 teaspoon chopped root ginger
$^1/_2$ teaspoon salt
$^1/_2$ cup salad oil

SALAD

250g bunch spinach
8 rashers bacon
6 hardboiled eggs
12 button mushrooms

DRESSING

Crush and peel garlic. Combine garlic, mustard, pepper, vinegar, ginger, salt and oil in a screw-top jar. Set aside until ready to use, then shake vigorously and pour over the salad.

SALAD

Wash spinach and remove stems. Carefully wrap leaves in absorbent paper and place in a plastic bag in refrigerator. Remove rind from bacon and cook until crisp. Roughly chop. Shell and slice the eggs. Wipe and slice the mushrooms. Arrange spinach on a large flat platter. Top with rows of sliced egg and mushrooms. Spoon bacon on top of egg. Pour dressing over and serve immediately.

Serves 6.

Special Salad (left), Chinese Vegetable Salad and Spinach and Egg Salad

SPECIAL SALAD

We always have roasted everything for dinner but when it comes to the greens a salad does us very well, especially with a red and green theme. Prepare all the ingredients and store in a plastic bag, refrigerated until ready to serve.

Mixed salad greens, such as buttercrunch
    lettuce, spinach

3 radishes

1 punnet strawberries

2 spring onions

1 red capsicum

2 tablespoons finely chopped coriander

½ cup vinaigrette

Wash and dry the salad greens. Break into bite-sized pieces. Place in a plastic bag. Wash, trim and grate the radishes. Wash the strawberries and halve if large. Trim the spring onions and cut on the diagonal. Deseed the red capsicum and cut the flesh into thin strips. Add the grated radishes, strawberries, spring onions, red capsicum and coriander to the lettuce. Pour over the vinaigrette just before serving. Toss to mix in the bag then arrange on a serving platter. Serve immediately.

Serves 6.

CHINESE VEGETABLE SALAD

300g snow peas

425g can baby corn

100g snow pea sprouts

1 tablespoon sesame oil

2 tablespoons soy sauce

1 teaspoon grated root ginger

1 tablespoon toasted sesame seeds

Wash snow peas. Top, tail and trim if necessary. Blanch in boiling water for 3 minutes. Drain and refresh in cold water. Drain well. Drain the baby corn. Mix the snow peas, corn and snow pea sprouts together. Shake the sesame oil, soy sauce and grated root ginger together in a screw-top jar. Pour over the vegetables and toss to coat. Sprinkle with sesame seeds.

Serves 4 to 6.

SWEET POTATO SALAD

3 medium sweet potatoes

4 spring onions

2 bananas

¼ cup lemon juice

½ cup low-fat sour cream

¼ cup mayonnaise

1 teaspoon curry powder

Salt

Freshly ground black pepper

1 tablespoon toasted sesame seeds

Peel sweet potatoes. Cut into pieces and steam or cook in boiling salted water for 15 minutes or until tender. Drain and leave to cool. Slice spring onions on the diagonal into 1cm pieces. Peel bananas and cut into ½ cm slices. Place in a bowl. Pour lemon juice over bananas and mix to coat. When sweet potatoes are cold, cut into cubes. Mix sweet potatoes, spring onions and bananas together. Mix sour cream, mayonnaise, curry powder, salt and freshly ground black pepper together. Carefully mix through the sweet potato mixture. Place in a serving bowl and garnish with sesame seeds.

Serves 3 to 4.

PEAR, WALNUT AND BLUE CHEESE SALAD

4 pears

¼ cup lemon juice

¼ cup walnut halves

100g wedge blue vein cheese

1 tablespoon vinaigrette

Peel the pears. Cut into quarters and remove the core. Cut pear quarters into 3 to 4 slices. Toss pears in lemon juice and drain. Break walnut halves in half. Cut cheese into 1cm cubes. Carefully mix pears, walnuts and cheese together. Place in a serving bowl and drizzle over vinaigrette.

Serves 4 to 5.

From top left clockwise: Sweet potato Salad, Tropical Salad, Sue's Banana Salad and Pear, Walnut and Blue Cheese Salad

TROPICAL SALAD

450g can pineapple pieces

425g can mango slices

3 spring onions

½ cup long thread coconut

3 tablespoons coconut cream

1 tablespoon lime juice

¼ teaspoon ground coriander

1 tablespoon fresh coriander or parsley

Drain the pineapple and mango. Cut mango into smaller pieces if necessary. Trim spring onions and cut into 1cm pieces on the diagonal. Mix the pineapple pieces, mango, spring onions and coconut together. Combine with the coconut cream, lime juice and ground coriander. Pour over the salad and toss to coat. Garnish with chopped coriander or parsley.

Serves 4.

SUE'S BANANA SALAD

4 medium bananas

2 onions

1 tablespoon oil

2 teaspoons curry powder

¼ cup cider vinegar

¼ cup sultanas

1 tablespoon finely chopped coriander

Peel and slice bananas and onions. Heat the oil in a frying pan and saute the onions for 5 minutes or until clear. Add the curry powder and cook for about 1 minute or until the spices smell fragrant. Add the bananas and vinegar and cook for 2 minutes. Remove from the heat. Stir in the sultanas and place in a serving dish. Leave until cold. Serve garnished with chopped coriander.

Serves 3 to 4.

DAYLIGHT SAVERS

With long summer evenings we often lose ourselves in the garden, mowing the lawns or walking on the beach.

That means we have to either be organised and have the evening meal sorted in advance or be adept at rustling up a delicious meal in super quick time so we don't end up eating when we have lost interest in food.

Simple and light ideas, or something a little more hearty, as a change from the usual barbecue summer fare, are offered in this chapter.

Mussel Sauce

400g fettuccine

24 to 32 fresh mussels

1 onion

2 cloves garlic

2 tablespoons extra virgin olive oil

$^1/_4$ cup lemon juice

400g can tomatoes in juice

2 tablespoons chilli sauce

Freshly ground black pepper

2 tablespoons chopped parsley

Cook pasta in boiling, salted water for 8 to 10 minutes, or until tender. Drain. Scrub and de-beard mussels. Peel onion and chop finely. Crush, peel and chop garlic. Heat oil in a large saucepan and saute onion and garlic for 5 minutes, or until onion is clear. Add lemon juice, tomatoes, chilli sauce, pepper and parsley. Bring to the boil. Add mussels. Cover and cook over a moderate heat for about 5 minutes. Mussel shells should open in this time. Discard any mussels that don't open. Remove mussels from shells for all but 8 mussels. Mix mussels into cooking liquid. Pour over cooked pasta. Garnish with mussels in shell.

Serves 4.

From back clockwise: Mussel Sauce, Simple Hot Smoked Salmon Sauce and Tuna Sauce

SIMPLE HOT SMOKED SALMON SAUCE

This is special treat fare. Hot smoked salmon looks cooked and is available from the deli section of the supermarket. Cold smoked salmon, on the other hand, looks translucent and uncooked. Both are delicious and both can be eaten straight from the packet. Canned salmon can be substituted as a cheaper option.

400g fettuccine
100g hot smoked salmon
2 cups natural unsweetened yoghurt
1 tablespoon whole seed mustard
2 tablespoons chopped fresh dill
Sprig dill

Cook pasta in boiling, salted water for 8 to 10 minutes, or until tender. Drain. Remove skin from salmon and break flesh into chunks. Mix salmon, yoghurt, mustard and chopped dill together in a saucepan. Bring almost to the boil. Pour over cooked fettuccine. Garnish with a sprig of dill.

Serves 4.

TUNA SAUCE

I always advocate keeping a can of fish in the store-cupboard. This is a great recipe to use that can of fish when you are caught short or have unexpected mouths to feed.

1 onion
50g butter
¼ cup flour
2 cups milk
185g can tuna in brine
2 tablespoons chopped parsley
1 teaspoon grated lemon rind
Salt
Freshly ground black pepper
400g tagliatelle
Lemon slices

Peel onion and chop finely. Melt butter in a saucepan. Add onion and saute for 5 minutes, or until clear. Remove from heat and stir in flour. Return to heat and cook until frothy. Slowly stir in milk. Cook, stirring, until sauce boils and thickens. Drain tuna. Add to sauce with parsley, lemon rind, salt and pepper. Simmer for 5 minutes. Cook pasta in boiling, salted water for 8 to 10 minutes, or until tender. Drain. Pour sauce over cooked pasta. Garnish with lemon slices.

Serves 4.

FISH PIE

1 large onion

1 cup milk

1 bay leaf

Freshly ground black pepper

1/4 cup flour

50g soft butter

500g smoked fish

TOPPING

2 medium potatoes

1 tablespoon butter

1 tablespoon milk

1 tablespoon chopped parsley

Peel and quarter onion. Place milk, onion, bay leaf and pepper in a saucepan and heat or microwave until boiling. Mix flour and butter to a smooth paste. Remove milk from heat and whisk in butter mixture. Return to heat and cook until sauce boils and thickens. Mix in smoked fish and heat through. Pour mixture into an ovenproof dish. Top with mashed potato topping. Grill until lightly golden.

TOPPING

Peel potatoes and cook in boiling salted water until tender. Drain all but two tablespoons of water. Mash potatoes in the water. Add butter, milk and parsley and whip with a fork until smooth and fluffy.

Serves 4.

SMOKED FISH BREAD PIES

300g smoked fish

1 onion

3 tablespoons butter

1/4 cup flour

1 1/4 cups milk

2 tomatoes

1 tablespoon chopped parsley or dill

Salt

Freshly ground black pepper

12 to 14 slices sandwich bread

Butter

1 tablespoon poppy seeds

Remove bones and skin from fish and flake. Peel onion and chop roughly. Melt butter in a saucepan and cook onion until clear. Stir in flour. Cook until frothy. Gradually add milk, stirring constantly until mixture boils and thickens. Roughly chop tomatoes. Add tomato, fish, parsley, salt and pepper to sauce. Cool. Remove crusts from bread and butter each slice on one side. Line the base and sides of four 10cm quiche or pie dishes with the bread, buttered side down, cutting to fit the sides. Divide the fish mixture evenly among the dishes. Cut lids from remaining bread and place on top of fish, buttered side up. Sprinkle with poppy seeds. Bake at 190°C for 20 minutes or until golden.

Makes 5.

Fish Pie and
Smoked Fish Bread Pies

SEAFOOD LASAGNE

350g fish such as smoked fish, barramundi, scallops, prawns, canned fish, or a combination of fish

2 spring onions

$1/2$ teaspoon grated lemon rind

1 tablespoon lemon juice

Freshly ground black pepper

400g spinach lasagne

$1/2$ cup grated mozzarella cheese

CHEESE SAUCE

50g butter

$1/4$ cup flour

$1^1/2$ cups milk

1 cup grated tasty cheese

Remove bones and cut fish into thin strips if necessary. If using canned fish, drain. Trim and slice spring onions. Mix fish, onions, lemon rind, lemon juice and pepper together. Oil a lasagne or ovenproof dish. Cut a sheet of lasagne to fit. Place in bottom of dish. Spread a third of the fish mixture over the lasagne. Top with a layer of lasagne then a layer of cheese sauce. Repeat the layers until the ingredients are all used, finishing with a layer of sauce. Sprinkle with mozzarella cheese. Bake at 180°C for 35 to 40 minutes, or until golden.

CHEESE SAUCE

Melt butter in a saucepan. Add flour and cook until frothy. Remove from heat and gradually add milk, stirring after each addition. Return to heat and cook until mixture boils and thickens. Stir in tasty cheese.

Serves 4.

Seafood Lasagne (top) and Summer Lasagne Squares

SUMMER LASAGNE SQUARES

This makes a great entree for a summer meal.

425g can Italian seasoned tomatoes
2 zucchini
200g egg lasagne
8 slices mozzarella cheese
8 to 10 fresh basil leaves
$^1/_2$ cup grated parmesan cheese

Heat tomatoes until boiling. Trim zucchini and cut into matchstick strips about 2mm wide. Add to tomatoes and cook for 5 minutes. Cut lasagne sheets into twelve 9cm squares. Cook squares in boiling water for 6 to 8 minutes. Place a square of lasagne on an individual serving plate. Spread with tomato mixture, top with mozzarella cheese and torn basil leaves. Top with another piece of lasagne, tomato mixture, basil and mozzarella cheese. Finish with a piece of lasagne and sprinkle with grated parmesan cheese. Serve immediately.

Serves 4.

ITALIAN PASTA PIE

Use any savoury pastry for this pie.

1 medium eggplant
Salt
3 cups cooked pasta
2 cups milk
$^1/_4$ cup flour
50g soft butter
3 eggs
Salt
Freshly ground black pepper
2 cups grated tasty cheese
3 zucchini
2 tomatoes
Fresh basil leaves
2 sheets flaky puff pastry

Cut eggplant into slices. Sprinkle both sides with salt. Stand for a few minutes while preparing rest of ingredients. Drain pasta well. Bring milk to the boil in a large saucepan. Mix flour and butter together. Remove milk from heat and stir in butter mixture. Cook until thick and boiling. Cool. Lightly beat eggs. Mix pasta, salt, pepper, grated cheese and eggs into sauce mixture. Trim zucchini and slice thinly. Slice tomatoes. Cut a piece of pastry to fit the bottom of a 20cm diameter deep cake tin. Prick bottom and bake at 200°C for 10 minutes. Spread half the cool pasta mixture on top of pastry round. Lay slices of zucchini, eggplant, tomato and basil leaves over pasta. Spread over remaining pasta mixture. Top with second pastry sheet. Trim to fit. Bake at 200°C for 10 to 15 minutes then reduce temperature to 180°C for 30 minutes or until golden and cooked. To serve, cut into wedges.

Serves 6.

Italian Pasta Pie

Glazed Pickled Pork with Redcurrant Sauce

1 piece pickled pork about 1kg

Hot water

GLAZE

2 tablespoons orange juice

3 tablespoons brown sugar

1 teaspoon prepared mustard

REDCURRANT SAUCE

$^1/_2$ cup redcurrant jelly

1 teaspoon grated orange rind

$^1/_4$ cup orange juice

1 teaspoon prepared mustard

Place pickled pork in crockpot. Cover with hot water. Cover and cook on high for 4 to 6 hours or low for 6 to 8 hours, or until cooked. Remove from crockpot and remove skin. Spread glaze over and place under a hot grill until golden. Serve with redcurrant sauce.

GLAZE

Mix orange juice, brown sugar and mustard together.

REDCURRANT SAUCE

Mix redcurrant jelly, orange rind, orange juice and mustard together in a saucepan. Bring to the boil and simmer for 5 minutes.

Serves 6.

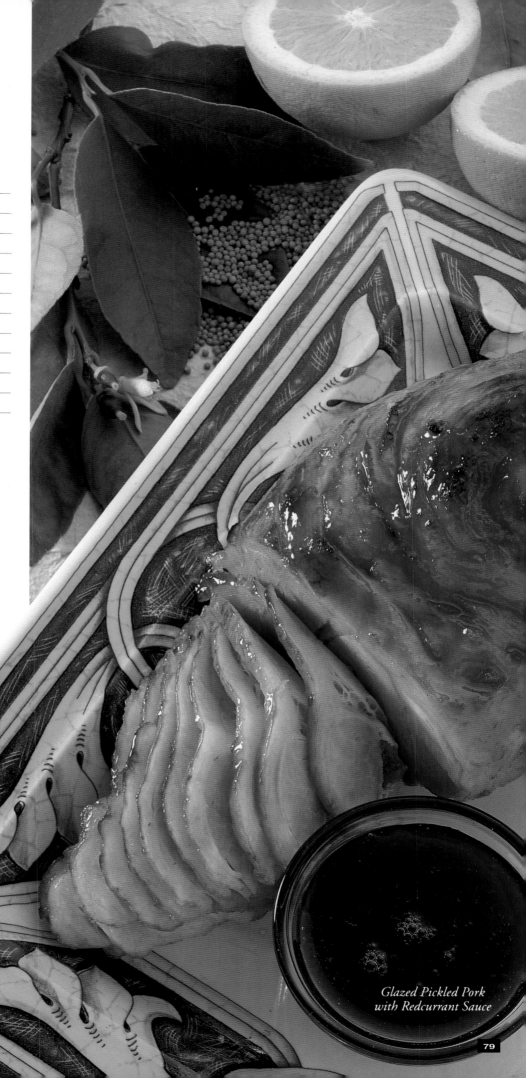

Glazed Pickled Pork with Redcurrant Sauce

CORNED BEEF WITH QUICK MUSTARD SAUCE

Cooking time will depend on the thickness of the meat. The corned beef won't spoil if it cooks for longer.

1 piece corned beef about 1 to 1.5kg

Hot water

1 tablespoon vinegar

2 tablespoons brown sugar

QUICK MUSTARD SAUCE

1/2 cup low-fat sour cream

1 tablespoon prepared whole seed mustard

2 teaspoons chopped fresh dill

Place corned beef in crockpot. Cover with hot water and add vinegar and brown sugar. Cover and cook on low for 6 to 8 hours. Drain and serve hot or cold with Quick Mustard Sauce.

QUICK MUSTARD SAUCE

Mix sour cream, mustard and dill together.

Serves 6 to 8.

TANGY CROCKPOT CHICKEN

Medium size chicken

2 cloves garlic

1 teaspoon grated lemon rind

25g butter

1 tablespoon chopped parsley

1 tablespoon honey

Remove giblets from chicken. Crush, peel and chop garlic. Mix garlic, lemon rind, butter, parsley and honey together. Carefully ease the skin away from the breast of the chicken. Spread half the butter mixture under the skin of the chicken and the other half over the chicken. Place chicken in crockpot. Cover and cook on low for 6 to 8 hours, or until the chicken juices run clear. If wished, the chicken can be grilled until golden before serving.

Serves 4 to 6.

HEARTY BEEF CASSEROLE

Use topside, skirt steak or gravy beef for this casserole depending on your budget.

500g chuck steak

1 onion

2 carrots

2 parsnips

2 potatoes

Freshly ground black pepper

1 cup hot water

2 beef stock cubes

1/4 cup sherry

1/4 cup tomato paste

2 tablespoons cornflour

2 tablespoons water

Trim fat from meat. Cut meat into 2cm cubes. Place in crockpot. Peel and chop onion. Scrub and dice carrots, parsnips and potatoes. Add to crockpot with pepper, hot water and crumbled stock cubes, sherry and tomato paste. Cover and cook on low for 9 to 11 hours. Mix cornflour and water together. Pour into crockpot and turn to high while preparing vegetables or salad to serve with the casserole.

Serves 4 to 6.

Tangy Crockpot Chicken, Corned Beef with Quick Mustard Sauce and Hearty Beef Casserole

FETTA AND RED CAPSICUM PIE

4 large red capsicums

75g butter

8 sheets filo pastry

250g spinach

200g fetta cheese

2 tablespoons unsweetened natural yoghurt

Freshly ground black pepper

2 teaspoons sesame seeds

Halve and deseed capsicums. Grill until skin is blackened and blistered. Cool and remove skin. Cut into quarters. Melt butter. Brush a sheet of filo pastry with melted butter. Place in a 20cm round cake tin. Repeat with another four sheets of pastry and melted butter, layering the pastry at right angles. Cover with a tea-towel. Remove stalks from spinach and blanch spinach leaves in boiling water for 2 to 3 minutes or until just limp. Pat dry with paper towels. Crumble fetta cheese. Place spinach at the bottom of the pie. Spread over yoghurt. Top with fetta cheese. Place capsicums on top. Grind over black pepper. Brush remaining three sheets of pastry with melted butter. Place pastry on top of vegetables. Fold over edges. Brush with melted butter. Sprinkle with sesame seeds. Bake at 180°C for 35 minutes or until golden.

Serves 4 to 6.

Fetta and Red Capsicum Pie and Cheese and Leek Flan

CHEESE AND LEEK FLAN

400g packet crusty pie pastry

2 medium leeks

1 tablespoon oil

500g pot cottage cheese with chives

1 cup natural unsweetened yoghurt

2 cups grated gruyere cheese

1 teaspoon wholeseed mustard

1 egg

Roll out pastry on a lightly floured board. Use to line a 21cm pie dish with a lip. Cut out pastry shapes with trimmings. Wet edge of pastry in dish and decorate with pastry shapes if wished. Trim leeks. Wash well and slice very thinly. Heat oil in a frying pan and saute leeks over a moderate heat for 5 minutes. Mix leeks, cottage cheese, yoghurt, cheese, mustard and egg together until well combined. Turn mixture into pastry case. Bake at 190°C for 20 to 25 minutes or until set. Serve hot or cold.

Serves 4 to 6.

MEXICAN CHICKEN FILLING

Use this filling for tacos, enchiladas or burritos.

4 spring onions

1 tablespoon oil

2 cups chopped cooked chicken

310g can whole kernel sweetcorn

1 teaspoon dried oregano

1 teaspoon Mexican chilli powder

Salt

Freshly ground black pepper

1/2 cup low fat sour cream

Trim spring onions and slice finely. Heat oil in a saucepan and saute onion for 2 to 3 minutes. Add chicken, drained corn, oregano, chilli powder, salt, pepper and sour cream and bring to the boil.

TACOS

Fill warm taco shells with Mexican Chicken Filling, grated cheese, shredded lettuce, tomato salsa and guacamole.

ENCHILADAS

Fry tortillas in oil on both sides until soft. Remove from pan and fill with Mexican Chicken Filling. Roll up and place in an ovenproof dish. Top with tomato salsa and grated cheese. Bake at 180°C for 10 minutes or until hot.

BURRITOS

Brush tortillas with melted butter. Heat in the oven or microwave until warm. Spread with hot Mexican Chicken Filling, shredded lettuce and tomato salsa. Roll up and serve immediately.

Makes 8.

Mexican Chicken Filling used in tacos (back) and burritos

THAI BEEF SALAD

I have given this salad recipe to many people and it has always been a success. Thai fish sauce is available from Asian specialty stores and a bottle will last a long time.

500g fillet steak in one piece

2 cloves garlic

1 tablespoon soy sauce

2 tablespoons lime juice

1 tablespoon Thai fish sauce

1 tablespoon sugar

2 tablespoons chopped fresh coriander

1 tablespoon chopped mint leaves

Lettuce leaves

3 to 4 spring onions

1 to 2 fresh chillies

Cherry tomatoes

Fresh coriander

Remove sinews and fat from meat. Cook in a non-stick frying pan until medium rare. Remove and leave until cold. Do not pierce the flesh. Use tongs to handle the meat. Crush and peel garlic. Place garlic, soy sauce, lime juice, fish sauce, sugar, first measure of coriander and mint leaves in a food processor. Process until smooth. Thinly slice beef. Toss beef in the garlic mixture. Arrange lettuce on a serving platter. Place the beef slices to one side. Arrange spring onions, chillies, cherry tomatoes and coriander on other side.

Serves 4 to 5.

MUSSEL SALAD

About 48 fresh mussels in the shell

4 spring onions

2 onions

1/2 cup malt vinegar

Pinch chilli powder

Salt and pepper

Steam mussels for about 5 minutes or until shells open. Discard any mussels that do not open. Remove mussels from shells and place in a bowl. Trim spring onions and slice thinly. Peel onions and cut into rings. Mix spring onions and onions into mussels. Pour vinegar over. Sprinkle over chilli powder, salt and pepper. Mix well. Cover and refrigerate for several hours before serving.

Serves 6.

TASTE OF SUMMER

MELON AND PROSCIUTTO SALAD

Serve this salad as an entree or a light summer luncheon dish with crusty French bread.

1 rock melon

20 slices prosciutto

1/4 cup vinaigrette

Freshly ground black pepper

Basil leaves

Cut melon in half and remove seeds. Cut into 12 wedges and peel. Cut wedges in half crosswise. Place melon on a serving platter. Curl prosciutto around melon. Drizzle over vinaigrette and coarsely grind over pepper. Garnish with basil leaves.

Serves 4.

LIME AND CORIANDER FISH SALAD

If prawns aren't in your budget leave them out or use a can of shrimps instead.

500g firm white fish fillets

6 cooked prawns

1 small red chilli

2 limes

1/4 cup very finely chopped green pepper

2 tablespoons olive oil

2 tablespoons lime juice

2 tablespoons chopped fresh coriander

Salad greens

Steam or microwave fish until cooked. Leave to cool. Cut into cubes. Shell prawns if necessary. Deseed chilli and cut flesh into very small pieces. Cut limes into eighths. Mix fish, chilli, limes and pepper together in a bowl. Mix oil, lime juice and coriander together. Pour over fish. Serve on a bed of salad greens. Arrange prawns on top.

Serves 4.

Thai Beef Salad, Melon and Prosciutto Salad, Lime and Coriander Fish Salad and Mussel Salad

PICNICS

With so many special outdoor things to do in our country, picnics are no longer confined to daytime events. Opera or symphony in the park, wonderful air displays at dusk and special firework displays have all given the picnic a new lease of life as we pack our basket and trek off to secure a good spot to view an evening of culture and fun.

Whatever your picnic requirements, it's always nice to make the effort to prepare something special as a change from the usual breadroll and cheese.

Make a pie, a special cake or a smart sandwich. There are plenty of things to choose from that will add to the enjoyment of your picnic.

BRUSCHETTA AND CROSTINI

Suit yourself on what you make. Both are delicious and make a useful base for all sorts of vegetables, spreads and toppings.

BRUSCHETTA

The original garlic bread

Thick slices of bread

1 clove garlic

Olive oil

Grill bread slices on both sides. Crush and peel garlic. Rub over the bread. Drizzle over olive oil. Use as wished.

CROSTINI

Small rounds or squares of bread

Olive oil or melted butter

Brush bread with olive oil or melted butter. Grill until lightly toasted or bake at 190°C for 5 minutes.

CREAMY EGGPLANT TOPPING

1 medium eggplant

3 cloves garlic

2 tablespoons olive oil

2 tablespoons lemon juice

Salt

Freshly ground black pepper

Bruschetta or crostini

Fresh basil leaves

Place eggplant on a baking tray with unpeeled garlic and grill under a hot grill, turning until eggplant is black on all sides. Take care not to puncture the eggplant. Turn garlic regularly and remove from grill if the skin starts to brown. When eggplant is black and soft remove from oven. Leave to cool. Peel away eggplant skin, drain if necessary and mash the flesh. Peel garlic and mash flesh with eggplant. Add olive oil, lemon juice, salt and pepper to eggplant puree. Mix well. Use to top bruschetta or crostini. Garnish with torn basil leaves.

Makes about 1^1/$_2$ cups.

Bruschetta and Crostini with Chilli Broccoli Spread, Creamy Eggplant Topping and Roasted Capsicum Topping.

CHILLI BROCCOLI SPREAD

3 cloves garlic

500g broccoli

1 tablespoon olive oil

¼ teaspoon chilli powder

¾ cup boiling water

Salt

Bruschetta or crostini

3 to 4 black olives

Crush and peel garlic and chop finely. Trim broccoli and cut into florets. Heat oil in a saucepan. Saute garlic over a low heat for 2 minutes. Add chilli powder and saute for a further 1 minute or until garlic and chilli are fragrant. Add broccoli, water and salt. Cover and cook over a medium heat for about 10 minutes or until broccoli is just cooked. Remove lid. Mash with a potato masher. Continue to cook over a low heat, mashing regularly, until water has evaporated and broccoli has formed a coarse puree. Use to top brushcetta or crostini and garnish with sliced black olives.

Makes 1½ cups.

ROASTED CAPSICUM TOPPING

2 red capsicums

1 yellow capsicum

1 green capsicum

1 clove garlic

1 tablespoon olive oil

1 tablespoon white vinegar

Freshly ground black pepper

Bruschetta or crostini

Cut capsicums in half lengthwise. Remove seeds and stems. Place cut-side down on an oven tray and grill until the skin is blistered and brown. Wrap in foil and leave to cool. Remove skins and cut flesh into thin strips. Crush and peel garlic and chop finely. Mix capsicum strips, garlic, oil, vinegar and pepper together. Use to top bruschetta or crostini.

Makes about 1½ cups.

TASTE OF SUMMER

ONION MARMALADE

Use balsamic vinegar for this if your budget runs to it.

6 medium onions
2 tablespoons brown sugar
1/2 cup chicken stock
1/2 cup red wine vinegar
2 tablespoons wholeseed mustard

Peel onions and slice finely. Place in a saucepan with the sugar and stock. Cook over a moderate heat for 15 minutes or until all the liquid has evaporated and the onions have become golden. Stir in the vinegar and mustard. Cook for a further 5 minutes. Serve on crostini, bruschetta or as an accompaniment to cold cuts.

Makes 2 cups.

VEGETABLE SUSHI

3 nori sheets
3 cups cooked cold short grain rice
2 tablespoons white vinegar
1 tablespoon sugar
1/4 teaspoon salt
2 medium carrots
1 zucchini
2 tablespoons white vinegar
3 tablespoons pickled ginger
Wasabi
Pickled ginger

Place nori sheets on a clean tea-towel. Combine rice, first measure of vinegar, sugar and salt. Divide rice among the nori sheets, spreading out to within 2cm of the edge. Peel or scrub carrots and grate finely. Trim zucchini and grate finely. Mix second measure of vinegar into carrots. Divide carrot among nori sheets and spread over rice. Spread grated zucchini over carrot. Place one tablespoon of pickled ginger down the centre of each sushi. Using the tea-towel as an aid, roll nori and filling to form a tight cylinder. Cut into 2cm wide slices. Serve with wasabi and extra pickled ginger.

Makes 30.

PUMPKIN AND CUMIN DIP

Pumpkins vary in dryness. If you have a dry pumpkin you may need to add more oil to make this dip dippable.

1 small butternut pumpkin

1 teaspoon ground cumin

1 teaspoon salt

2 tablespoons crunchy peanut butter

$1/2$ teaspoon chilli powder

1 tablespoon oil

2 tablespoons chopped roasted peanuts

Place pumpkin in an ovenproof dish. Roast at 190°C for about 1 hour or until cooked through. Cool slightly then remove the top. Scoop out the seeds and discard. Scoop out flesh of pumpkin and mash with the cumin, salt, peanut butter, chilli powder and oil. Place pumpkin mixture back in pumpkin shell. Sprinkle peanuts over pumpkin. Refrigerate until ready to serve.

Makes about 2 cups

ROASTED CAPSICUM AND SUNDRIED TOMATO PATE

2 large red capsicums

5cm piece root ginger

$1/2$ cup chopped sundried tomatoes in oil

250g cream cheese

Cut the capsicums in half lengthwise. Remove seeds and stem. Place cut-side down on an oven tray and grill or fan grill until the skins are blistered and brown. Remove from oven and wrap in foil. Leave to cool. When cool enough to handle, remove the skins. Grate ginger. Place capsicum halves, sundried tomatoes and grated ginger in a food processor. Add cream cheese and process to form a smooth paste. Place in a dish and chill until needed.

Makes about 2 cups.

Roasted Capsicum and Sundried Tomato Pate, Pumpkin and Cumin Dip, Onion Marmalade and Vegetable Sushi.

TASTE OF SUMMER

PIZZA DOUGH

Tepid water is used in yeast cookery. The water is this temperature when a few drops on the back of the hand feel neither warm or cold.

$1/2$ teaspoon sugar
$1/2$ cup tepid water
$1^1/2$ teaspoons dried yeast
1 - $1^1/4$ cups flour suitable for breadmaking
$1/2$ teaspoon salt
1 tablespoon extra virgin olive oil

Dissolve sugar in water. Sprinkle yeast over water and leave for about 10 minutes or until frothy. Place 1 cup of flour into a mixing bowl with the salt. Make a well in the centre and add the oil and yeast mixture. Mix to combine. Knead dough on a lightly floured surface until smooth and elastic, adding extra flour if necessary. Shape into a ball and place in a lightly greased bowl. Turn dough over. Cover and leave in a warm place until double in bulk. Punch dough down and knead lightly. Use to make pizza with toppings of your choice, pizza bread or calzone.

Makes enough dough for a 30cm diameter pizza.

PIZZETTES

These are great to serve with drinks. Any leftovers make a good lunchbox addition.

1 quantity pizza dough or quick pizza dough
$1/2$ cup fresh pesto sauce
Slices mozzarella
36 slices tomato
Freshly ground black pepper

Cut the pizza dough in half. Divide each half into 18 portions. Make each portion into a 4cm diameter round. Brush with pesto, top with mozzarella and a tomato slice. Grind over black pepper. Bake at 200°C for 10 minutes or until pizzettes are cooked.

Makes 36.

QUICK PIZZA DOUGH

This pizza dough has all the flavour of a traditional yeast dough but requires no rising.

1 teaspoon sugar
$^1/_2$ cup tepid water
$1^1/_2$ teaspoons dried yeast
1 cup self-raising flour
$^1/_2$ cup flour suitable for breadmaking
$^1/_4$ teaspoon salt
1 tablespoon extra virgin olive oil

Dissolve the sugar in water. Sprinkle the yeast over the water and leave for 10 minutes or until frothy. Mix the self-raising flour, flour and salt together in a bowl. Make a well in the centre and add the olive oil and yeast mixture. Mix well, adding extra flour if necessary. Knead on a floured board until smooth and elastic, adding more flour if necessary. Use to make pizza with toppings of your choice, pizza bread or calzone.

Makes enough dough for a 30cm diameter pizza.

POSH PIZZA

1 quantity pizza dough or quick pizza dough
$^1/_4$ cup tomato paste
$^1/_4$ cup pesto sauce
50g hot smoked salmon
3 tablespoon extra virgin olive oil
$^1/_4$ cup shaved or grated parmesan cheese

Roll dough to a 24cm diameter circle or to fit a 20cm x 30cm sponge roll tin. Combine tomato paste and pesto and spread over the pizza base. Break the smoked salmon into pieces and arrange over the base. Drizzle with olive oil and top with parmesan cheese. Bake at 200°C for 15 minutes or until the pizza is golden. Cut into squares, wedges or fingers to serve as finger food or a light meal.

Serves 4.

Pizzettes (far left) & Posh Pizza (left)

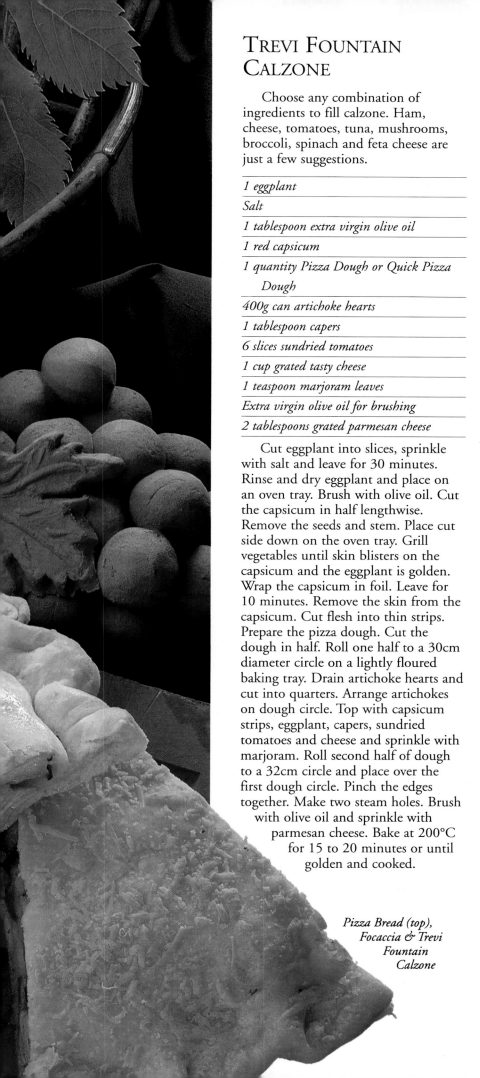

TREVI FOUNTAIN CALZONE

Choose any combination of ingredients to fill calzone. Ham, cheese, tomatoes, tuna, mushrooms, broccoli, spinach and feta cheese are just a few suggestions.

1 eggplant
Salt
1 tablespoon extra virgin olive oil
1 red capsicum
1 quantity Pizza Dough or Quick Pizza Dough
400g can artichoke hearts
1 tablespoon capers
6 slices sundried tomatoes
1 cup grated tasty cheese
1 teaspoon marjoram leaves
Extra virgin olive oil for brushing
2 tablespoons grated parmesan cheese

Cut eggplant into slices, sprinkle with salt and leave for 30 minutes. Rinse and dry eggplant and place on an oven tray. Brush with olive oil. Cut the capsicum in half lengthwise. Remove the seeds and stem. Place cut side down on the oven tray. Grill vegetables until skin blisters on the capsicum and the eggplant is golden. Wrap the capsicum in foil. Leave for 10 minutes. Remove the skin from the capsicum. Cut flesh into thin strips. Prepare the pizza dough. Cut the dough in half. Roll one half to a 30cm diameter circle on a lightly floured baking tray. Drain artichoke hearts and cut into quarters. Arrange artichokes on dough circle. Top with capsicum strips, eggplant, capers, sundried tomatoes and cheese and sprinkle with marjoram. Roll second half of dough to a 32cm circle and place over the first dough circle. Pinch the edges together. Make two steam holes. Brush with olive oil and sprinkle with parmesan cheese. Bake at 200°C for 15 to 20 minutes or until golden and cooked.

Pizza Bread (top), Focaccia & Trevi Fountain Calzone

FOCACCIA

Tepid water is blood heat, when a drop on the back of the hand feels neither hot nor cold. If you have a mixer with a dough hook, use this to do the mixing and kneading of this or any of the breads in this chapter.

1/2 teaspoon sugar
150ml tepid water
2 teaspoons dried yeast
2 cups flour suitable for breadmaking
1 tablespoon extra virgin olive oil
1 tablespoon rosemary leaves
1 tablespoon rock salt

Dissolve the sugar in the water. Sprinkle the yeast over. Leave for about 10 minutes or until frothy. Place the flour in a large bowl. Make a well in the centre. Pour in the yeast mixture and the olive oil. Mix until combined. Turn onto a lightly floured surface and knead until smooth and elastic. Turn dough into an oiled mixing bowl. Turn dough over. Cover with plastic wrap and leave in a warm place until doubled in bulk. Turn dough onto a lightly floured oven tray and roll dough to a 1 1/2 cm thick rectangle. Brush dough with extra olive oil, sprinkle with rosemary and rock salt. Using fingertips, dimple the surface of the focaccia. Cover and leave in a warm place until doubled in bulk. Bake at 230°C for 15 to 20 minutes or until golden and cooked.

Serves 6.

PIZZA BREAD

1 quantity pizza dough or quick pizza dough
3 tablespoons extra virgin olive oil
TOPPING
Extra virgin olive oil
3 cloves garlic
Rock salt

Divide the pizza dough in half. Roll each half into a 15cm diameter circle. Place on an oiled oven tray. Brush with olive oil. Crush, peel and finely chop the garlic. Sprinkle over the pizza dough and grind a little rock salt over. Bake at 200°C for 10 to 15 minutes or until golden and crisp. Cut into wedges.

Serves 6.

FARMHOUSE PIE

400g packet flaky puff pastry
4 rashers bacon
5 eggs
440g can cream style corn
1/4 cup chopped parsley
1 cup chopped cooked chicken
1/4 cup milk
1 teaspoon wholegrain mustard
Salt
Freshly ground black pepper
1 egg yolk
1 tablespoon water

Roll pastry out on a lightly floured board to 2mm thickness. Use to line the base and sides of a 20cm loose-bottomed cake tin. Derind bacon and chop flesh. Cook bacon lightly then set aside. In a mixing bowl beat together eggs, corn, parsley, chicken, milk and mustard. Stir in bacon and season to taste with salt and freshly ground black pepper. Pour filling into prepared tin. Re-roll remaining pastry and use to make a lid. Place on top of pie and seal edges. Mix egg yolk and water together. Brush over pastry top. Place on an oven tray. Bake at 200°C for 15 minutes then reduce temperature to 180°C for about 1¼ hours or until filling is set. Serve hot or cold.

Serves 8.

From front left clockwise: Farmhouse Pie, Bacon and Egg Pie and Chicken Pie

BACON AND EGG PIE

400g packet flaky puff pastry

4 eggs

4 rashers bacon

2 tomatoes

340g can asparagus spears

Roll out pastry on a lightly floured board to 2mm thickness. Line a 20cm square cake tin or a 35 x 11cm rectangular tin with the pastry, slashing and sealing on corners to make pastry fit. Re-roll remaining pastry for the top. Break eggs into pastry. Prick yolks. Derind bacon and chop roughly. Add to pastry shell. Slice tomatoes and lay over egg mixture. Drain asparagus and arrange spears over tomato. Grind over black pepper. Place pastry top over pie. Trim edges and crimp to seal. Cut two holes in top of pastry. Bake at 200°C for 30 to 40 minutes or until pastry is golden and filling set. Serve hot or cold.

Serves 4 to 6.

CHICKEN PIE

Use one cup of cold white sauce or natural unsweetened yoghurt instead of the sour cream in this dish if wished.

2 sheets flaky puff pastry

1 onion

1 tablespoon oil

1 tablespoon wholeseed mustard

1 teaspoon dried tarragon

250g pot low fat sour cream

Salt

Freshly ground black pepper

2 cups chopped cooked chicken

1 egg yolk

1 tablespoon water

1 tablespoon sesame seeds

Place one sheet of pastry in a 13cm pie dish or cake tin. Peel onion and chop finely. Heat oil in a frying pan and saute onion for 5 minutes or until clear. Mix onion, mustard, tarragon, sour cream, salt, pepper and chicken together. Fill pastry case in pie dish with this mixture. Wet edges of pastry. Place second sheet of pastry on top with points to the centre of each side of base pastry. Press edges together. Beat egg yolk and water together. Brush over surface of pastry, taking care not to brush over edges of pastry. Sprinkle with sesame seeds. Cut two steam holes in top of pie. Bake at 200°C for 15 to 20 minutes or until golden and cooked. Serve hot or cold.

Serves 3 to 4.

ITALIAN SAUSAGE DODADS

400g packet crusty pie pastry
60g mozzarella cheese
18 to 20 fresh basil leaves
1/2 cup prepared pasta sauce
1 egg
1 tablespoon water
3 tablespoons grated parmesan cheese

Cut pastry into rounds using a pastry cutter or a glass. Cut mozzarella into 1cm cubes. Place a cheese cube, basil leaf and a teaspoonful of pasta sauce in the middle of each pastry round. Wet pastry edges with water. Press pastry edges together in a pleated pattern. Lightly beat egg and water together. Brush over pastries. Cut two small holes in each pastry for steam to escape. Sprinkle with parmesan cheese. Bake at 190°C for 10 to 15 minutes or until pastries are golden and cooked. Serve warm.

Makes 18 to 20.

*Fruity Sausage Rolls,
Italian Sausage Dodads
and Cherry Hos*

FRUITY SAUSAGE ROLLS

1/2 cup grated green skinned apple
1/2 cup drained crushed pineapple
1/2 cup soft breadcrumbs
200g sausagemeat
370g roll flaky puff pastry
1 egg
1 tablespoon water
1 tablespoon sesame seeds

Mix apple, pineapple, breadcrumbs and sausagemeat together until well combined. Unroll pastry and cut in half lengthwise. Form half the sausagemeat mixture into a long tube with floured hands or use a piping bag without a nozzle to pipe a tube of sausagemeat along the centre of each piece of pastry. Wet one pastry edge. Roll pastry over sausagemeat and seal. Beat egg and water together and brush over sausage rolls. Cut into 4cm pieces. Cut two slashes in top of rolls and place on a baking tray. Sprinkle with sesame seeds. Bake at 200°C for 25 minutes or until golden and cooked.

Makes 15.

CHERRY HOS

Cocktail sausages can be used for these if wished but frankfurters are a little more sophisticated.

6 frankfurters
2 teaspoons prepared American mustard
1 sheet flaky puff pastry

Cut frankfurters in half. Spread the outside of each piece with mustard. Cut pastry sheets into 1cm strips. Wrap each piece of frankfurter with pastry starting at one end and winding it round until the frankfurter is covered. Wet the end of the pastry and seal the end. Bake at 200°C for 10 minutes or until golden.

Makes 12.

Savoury Pastry Bites

TASTE OF SUMMER

ROASTED GARLIC, CHICKEN AND RED CAPSICUM SLICE

2 sheets flaky puff pastry
8 cloves roasted garlic
1 tablespoon oil
250g chicken tenderloins
1 tablespoon chopped parsley
Strips of roasted red capsicum

Lay a sheet of pastry on an oven tray. Wet edges. Cut second sheet into 1¹/₂cm strips. Place a strip of pastry along each edge of pastry sheet, trimming to fit. Brush top of strips with water and repeat with remaining pastry strips. Prick bottom with a fork. Bake at 200°C for 10 to 15 minutes or until golden. Cool. Remove skin from garlic. Remove garlic pulp and mash. Spread over inside of pastry shell. Heat oil in a frying pan and fry chicken until cooked. Place chicken in pastry case. Sprinkle with chopped parsley and garnish with roasted capsicum slices. To serve, cut into slices.

TO ROAST GARLIC

Bake garlic at 180°C for 30 minutes.

Serves 4.

PUMPKIN FILO PARCELS

1 cup cold cooked mashed pumpkin
1 teaspoon cumin
1 egg
1 tablespoon finely chopped chives
16 sheets filo pastry
Melted butter

Mix pumpkin, cumin and egg together until well combined. Mix in chives. Cut each sheet of pasty in half. Brush each sheet with melted butter. Stack four halves on top of each other. Place two tablespoonfuls of the pumpkin mixture on each square. Brush pastry edges with melted butter and draw together, pressing to seal. Place on an oven tray and bake at 200°C for 10 to 15 minutes or until golden.

Makes 8.

Roasted Garlic, Chicken and Red Capsicum Slice and Pumpkin Filo Parcels

FINGER QUICHES

Use fresh or canned smoked fish for these savouries.

2 sheets flaky puff pastry
3 eggs
1/2 cup natural unsweetened yoghurt
1 tablespoon horseradish cream
1 cup finely chopped smoked fish
1 tablespoon chopped parsley

Cut pastry into 6cm rounds using a pastry cutter or a glass. Use to line mini muffin tins. Lightly beat eggs and yoghurt together. Mix in horseradish cream, smoked fish and parsley. Three-quarter fill each pastry case with the fish mixture. Bake at 190°C for 15 minutes or until filling is set and pastry cooked. Serve warm or cold.

Makes 24.

QUICK CHICKEN PIES

This is a great way to use leftover chicken. Make bigger versions if wished.

3 sheets flaky puff pastry
1 onion
1 tablespoon oil
1 tablespoon wholeseed mustard
2 tablespoons chopped parsley
1 cup chopped cooked chicken
1/2 cup low fat sour cream
1 egg
1 tablespoon water
1 tablespoon sesame seeds

Cut pastry sheets into quarters. Peel onion and finely chop. Heat oil in a frying pan and saute onion for 5 minutes or until clear. Mix onion, mustard, parsley, chicken and sour cream together. Place one tablespoonful of mixture in the centre of each pastry square. Brush edges of pastry with water. Fold corner to corner to form a triangle. Seal edges by pressing together. Mix egg and water together. Cut two slashes in the top of the triangles. Brush with egg wash. Sprinkle with sesame seeds. Bake at 200°C for 15 minutes or until golden.

Makes 12.

Finger Quiches and Quick Chicken Pies

IN THE
NTRY

lay in the garden can mean a

eding something done with it.

hutney or bottling that you are

a meal of fresh vegetables to

f summer produce, make it into

d later in the year.

HE GARDEN

TASTE OF SUMMER

MIXED BERRY JAM

Cherries can be used in this jam if wished. Use at least 3 different fruit types for this recipe and use in roughly equal amounts.

1kg mixed soft berry fruits such as strawberries, raspberries, red currants, gooseberries, boysenberries

1kg sugar

Prepare fruit according to type. In a large saucepan place the firmest of the mixed fruit. Place other fruits on top and heat very gently until juices run, then simmer until all the fruits are soft. Stir occasionally. Add sugar and stir in until dissolved. Boil steadily for about 10 minutes or until the jam gives a setting test. Place into hot, clean, dry jars and seal when cold.

Makes about 4 cups.

APRICOT JAM

For an almondy flavour to your apricot jam, crack 6 to 8 almond stones, remove the kernels and add these to the syrup with the apricot flesh.

1kg sugar

1 cup water

1kg apricots

Place the sugar and water in a large saucepan or preserving pan and heat gently, stirring frequently until mixture comes to the boil. Boil for 2 minutes. Wash and slice apricots, discarding stones, and put fruit into syrup. Boil for about 35 minutes or until the jam gives a setting test. Stir occasionally during boiling. Pour into hot, clean, dry jars and seal when cold.

Makes about 7 cups.

Mixed Berry Jam and Apricot Jam.

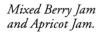

BLACKCURRANT JAM

1kg blackcurrants

1.5 litres water

6 cups sugar

Strip the blackcurrants from the stalks and place in a large saucepan or preserving pan with the water. Bring to the boil and cook fruit until it is soft, about 45 minutes. Add sugar and stir until dissolved. Return to the boil and boil briskly for about 25 minutes or until the jam gives a setting test. Pour into hot, clean, dry jars. Seal when cold.

Makes about 6 cups.

PLUM JAM

1kg plums

1 cup water

3¹/₂ cups sugar

Wash fruit and remove stones. Halve or slice fruit and place in a large saucepan or preserving pan. Bring to the boil and cook until fruit is soft. Add sugar and stir in until dissolved. Boil steadily for about 15 minutes until the jam gives a setting test. The cooking time will depend on the type of plums used.

Makes about 4 cups.

BOYSENBERRY AND PORT JAM

This is a good way to use up some port you may have hiding in your liquor cupboard. If you don't want a port flavour, leave it out of the jam.

1kg fresh or frozen boysenberries

3 cups sugar

¹/₄ cup port

Place the boysenberries in a large saucepan. If using frozen boysenberries, thaw over a low heat. Add the sugar and stir until sugar dissolves. Heat until mixture boils. Boil for about 7 to 10 minutes or until the jam gives a setting test. Pour into hot, clean, dry jars. Seal when cold.

Makes about 4 cups.

Plum Jam, Blackcurrant Jam in a sponge and Boysenberry and Port Jam in muffins.

TASTE OF SUMMER

BLACKBERRY AND ORANGE JAM

2 sweet oranges

650g tart apples

3 cups water

750g blackberries

3 cups sugar

Thinly pare the yellow rind from the oranges and tie in muslin. Squeeze the juice from the oranges and scrape out the pulp, but avoid any pith. Peel, core and chop apples. Place the washed blackberries, apple, orange juice and pulp, rinds and water in a large saucepan or preserving pan and bring to the boil. Boil steadily until all fruit is soft. Remove and discard the rinds. Cool until easy to handle, then measure and allow $^3/_4$ cup of sugar for each 1 cup of pulp. Add sugar and stir to dissolve, then boil briskly for about 15 minutes or until jam gives a setting test. Pour into hot, clean, dry jars and seal when cold.

Makes about 6 cups.

BLUEBERRY JAM

3 Granny Smith apples

$^1/_4$ cup lemon juice

3 cups blueberries

4 cups sugar

Peel apples. Core and slice thinly. Place apples, lemon juice and blueberries in a large saucepan. Bring to the boil and cook until blueberries are soft. Stir in sugar. Boil until jam gives a setting test. Pour into hot, clean, dry jars. Seal when cold.

Makes about 4 cups.

Blackberry and Orange Jam (top), and Blueberry Jam.

TASTE OF
SUMMER

RASPBERRY JAM

700g fresh or frozen raspberries

4¹/₂ cups sugar

3 tablespoons lemon juice

If using fresh fruit, clean and remove hulls. Place fresh or frozen fruit in a large saucepan and bring to the boil. Gently stir in sugar, stirring until dissolved. Add lemon juice and boil for about 5 minutes or until jam gives a setting test. Pour into hot, clean, dry jars. Seal when cold.

Makes 4 cups.

BASIL JELLY

Make the most of fresh summer basil with this delicious jelly.

6 Granny Smith apples

4 cups water

1¹/₂ cups sugar

¹/₄ cup fresh basil

Remove stems and blossom ends from apples. Chop apples roughly. Place apples and water in a large saucepan. Cover and cook for about 15 minutes or until soft. Pour apple mixture into a jelly bag over a bowl and leave until juice has dripped through. Resist the temptation to squeeze the bag as this will cause the jelly to become cloudy. Mix the juice and sugar together in a clean saucepan. Add the basil leaves and bring the mixture to the boil. Boil rapidly until the jelly gives a setting test. Remove from heat and using tongs remove basil and discard. Pour jelly into hot, clean, dry jars. Seal when cold.

Makes about 2 cups.

Basil Jelly served with cold cuts, and a jam roll filled with Raspberry Jam.

TASTE OF
SUMMER

MEXICAN TOMATO PICKLE

Serve this as an accompaniment for nachos or other Mexican dishes or use with cold meats or as a sandwich spread.

1kg tomatoes

6 cloves garlic

2 tablespoons oil

2 tablespoons ground cumin

2 tablespoons ground coriander

2 tablespoons prepared chilli

2 teaspoons salt

³/₄ cup wine vinegar

Peel tomatoes by blanching in boiling water for 1 minute then plunging into cold water. The skins will then come off easily. Chop tomatoes roughly, removing the core. Crush, peel and chop the garlic. Heat the oil in a large saucepan and fry the cumin and coriander, garlic and prepared chilli for 1 minute or until the spices smell fragrant. Add the tomatoes, salt and vinegar and simmer for about 1¹/₂ hours or until the pickle is thick. Pour into hot, clean, dry jars and seal when cold.

Makes 2¹/₂ cups.

PICKLED CHILLIES

Use these chillies in any dish that will be enhanced by their flavour.

1 cup white vinegar

¹/₂ cup safflower oil

2 teaspoons freshly ground black pepper

10 chillies

Mix vinegar, oil and pepper together in a medium-sized saucepan. Bring to the boil. Wash and dry the chillies and add to the pan. Bring to the boil and boil for 3 minutes. Spoon chillies into hot, clean, dry jars. Pour over the liquid and seal.

Makes about 1 cup.

Mexican Tomato Pickle served with nachos and Pickled Chillies served with tortillas.

119

ANNABELLE'S BREAD AND BUTTER PICKLES

When fellow food writer and good friend Annabelle White and I went seeking fresh produce in the country, we cooked up this treat over a glass of wine afterwards. It is very scrumptious.

8 cups sliced cucumbers or large gherkins

4 onions

4 mixed red, green and yellow capsicums

1 cup salt

2 litres cold water

2 cups white vinegar

2 cups sugar

2 teaspoons yellow mustard seeds

1 teaspoon pickling spice

2 teaspoons turmeric

2 teaspoons celery seed

$1/4$ teaspoon cinnamon

Place the cucumbers in a large non-metallic bowl. Peel and slice the onions. Deseed and slice the capsicums. Add onions and capsicums to the cucumbers. Sprinkle over the salt and add the cold water. Leave to stand for 3 hours. Drain but do not rinse. Mix the vinegar, sugar, mustard seeds, pickling spice, turmeric, celery seed and cinnamon together. Bring to the boil. Add vegetables. Bring to the boil. Simmer for 1 minute. Pack into hot, clean, dry jars. Seal with non-metallic lids.

Makes about 14 cups.

Annabelle's Bread and Butter Pickles.

TASTE OF SUMMER

ITALIAN TOMATO SAUCE

3kg ripe tomatoes

3 onions

8 large cloves garlic

$1/4$ cup olive oil

$3/4$ cup finely chopped fresh basil

1 teaspoon freshly ground black pepper

1 teaspoon salt

$1/4$ cup finely chopped parsley

Blanch tomatoes in boiling water for 1 minute then plunge into cold water. Remove skins and roughly chop flesh. Peel onions and chop. Crush, peel and chop garlic. Heat the first measure of oil in a large saucepan. Cook onions and garlic over a medium heat for about 5 minutes or until clear. Add tomatoes, basil, pepper and salt. Cook slowly for 1 to $1^1/4$ hours or until the sauce is thick. Stir in the parsley and cook for a further 5 minutes. Pour into freezer containers. Cover and freeze when cold

Makes about 8 cups.

TOMATO SAUCE

This recipe may be doubled if wished.

2kg ripe tomatoes
250g apples
2 large onions
5 cloves garlic
$^1/_4$ teaspoon cayenne pepper
1 teaspoon black pepper
$^1/_4$ teaspoon ground allspice
$^1/_2$ teaspoon ground cloves
$^3/_4$ cup sugar
$2^3/_4$ cups malt vinegar
1 teaspoon salt

Roughly chop tomatoes and place in a large saucepan. Core and roughly chop the apples. Peel and chop the onions. Crush, peel and chop the garlic. Add apples, onions, garlic, cayenne pepper, black pepper, allspice, cloves, sugar, vinegar and salt to the tomatoes. Cook over moderate heat until fruit and vegetables are tender. Cool slightly, then place in a blender or food processor. Return tomato mixture to saucepan. Boil gently for about 1 hour, stirring occasionally. When the sauce is thick, pour into hot, clean, dry bottles and seal when cold. For a smoother sauce, pass sauce through a sieve. Bring to the boil again before bottling in hot, clean, dry bottles.

Makes about 4 cups.

Italian Tomato Sauce served with pasta and Tomato Sauce served with sausages.

GHERKINS

1kg gherkins

$^1/_4$ cup salt

6 cloves garlic

$3^1/_2$ cups white vinegar

$^1/_2$ cup sugar

2 teaspoons yellow mustard seeds

Sprigs dill

Wash gherkins, rubbing off any prickles. Place in a non-metallic bowl and sprinkle with salt. Leave overnight. Drain gherkins. Crush and peel garlic. Place the vinegar, sugar, garlic and mustard seed in a large saucepan. Bring to the boil. Add the gherkins and simmer for 5 to 10 minutes or until tender. Cooking time will depend on the size of the gherkins. Pack gherkins into hot, clean, dry jars. Add a sprig of dill to each jar and a few mustard seeds. Bring liquid back to the boil and pour over the gherkins, making sure the gherkins are covered with the liquid. Cover with non-metallic lids. Resist for several weeks before using.

Makes about 8 cups.

FROZEN TOMATO PUREE

When tomatoes are cheap or you have a good crop in the garden, making your own puree is a good way to make sure you have plentiful supplies of this invaluable fruit for use later in the year. Freezing is the best way to deal with a large crop.

1kg tomatoes

$^1/_2$ teaspoon salt

1 teaspoon sugar

Blanch tomatoes in boiling water for 1 minute. Drain and plunge into cold water. Remove skins and cut out stem end. Chop roughly and place in a blender or food processor. Blend until pureed. Place in a saucepan and bring to the boil. Stir in salt and sugar. Boil slowly for 15 minutes or until thick. Cool then pack into freezer containers. Cover and freeze. When frozen, empty puree into plastic bags if wished.

Makes about $1^1/_2$ cups.

Gherkins, and Frozen Tomato Puree used to make tomato soup.

FRANCIS STREET CUCUMBER AND MINT PICKLE

1 large cucumber

2 onions

1 cup drained, crushed pineapple

$^3/_4$ cup sugar

1 cup white vinegar

$1^1/_2$ teaspoons salt

$2^1/_2$ teaspoons hot curry powder

$^1/_2$ teaspoon celery seed

$^1/_4$ cup chopped fresh mint

1 tablespoon cornflour

1 tablespoon water

Cut unpeeled cucumber lengthwise. Scoop out seeds and discard. Cut cucumber into thin slices. Peel and slice onions. Place cucumber, pineapple, onion, sugar, vinegar, salt, curry powder, celery seed and mint in a saucepan. Bring to the boil and cook uncovered for 20 minutes or until thick. Mix cornflour and water to a paste and stir into cucumber mixture. Bring to the boil and cook, stirring, until thickened. Pour into hot, clean, dry jars and seal when cold.

Makes about 2 cups.

Francis Street Cucumber and Mint Pickle.

BRANDIED APRICOTS

You can use this method of preserving for any summer fruit. They make a delicious dessert served with cream.

2kg firm ripe apricots
1/2 cup water
3/4 cup raw sugar
3/4 cup brandy

Cut apricots in half and remove stones. Place the water in a medium saucepan and add the sugar. Bring to the boil, stirring until sugar dissolves. Add the apricots and cook for 5 minutes or until the apricots are cooked but still hold their shape. Remove from heat. Cool slightly then stir in brandy. Pack into hot, clean, dry jars. Fill to the brim with the syrup. Make sure the rim is clean, then cover with a seal. Screw on a ring-band and leave until cold. The lid should be concave if sealed properly. Remove the band. Resist for several weeks before using.

Makes about 4 cups.

PICKLED PEACHES

These are the sort of thing that look terrific when photographed in glossy magazines. They taste terrific too. Serve with meat or pork dishes and salads.

12 medium-sized peaches
2 cups white vinegar
2 cups sugar
2 cinnamon sticks
1/4 cup whole cloves

Peel peaches and leave whole. Place vinegar, sugar, cinnamon and cloves in a saucepan and bring to the boil, stirring until sugar has dissolved. Carefully place peaches into the boiling syrup and cook gently for about 5 minutes or until peaches are just tender. Spoon peaches into hot, clean, dry jars. Pour over the syrup, filling the jar to the brim. Make sure the rim is clean, then cover with a seal. Screw on a ring-band and leave until cold. The lid should be concave if sealed properly. Remove band. Resist for several weeks before using.

Makes about 8 cups

Brandied Apricots for dessert and Pickled Peaches to serve with cooked meats and salads.

TASTE OF
SUMMER

Pickled Beetroot and Red Pepper Jelly.

PICKLED BEETROOT

You either love or loathe beetroot. For me, I detest the smell of them cooking but always enjoy eating them, especially like this.

1kg small beetroot

1 cup sugar

3 cups malt vinegar

1 cup water

1 teaspoon black peppercorns

6 whole cloves

Wash beetroot and cut off leaves, leaving about 2cm of the tops. Leave root ends intact. Cook in boiling water for 25 minutes or until tender. Drain. Rub off the skins and trim the ends. If the beetroot are large, cut into slices. Combine sugar, vinegar, water, peppercorns and cloves in a saucepan. Bring to the boil. Add beetroot and bring back to the boil. Pack beetroot into hot, clean, dry preserving jars. Pour over cooking liquid to the brim of the jar. Make sure rim is clean, then cover with a seal. Screw on a ring-band and leave until cold. The lid should be concave if sealed properly. Remove band. Store in a cool, dark place.
Makes about 4 cups

RED CAPSICUM JELLY

This is a really smart preserve. Delicious with something as simple as bread and cheese or as an accompaniment to grilled or barbecued meats. It's particularly good with chicken and lamb.

6 large red capsicums

3 cups cider vinegar

8 cups sugar

1 cup liquid pectin

Cut capsicums in half. Remove seeds and cut flesh into pieces. Chop finely in a blender, food processor or with a knife. Place in a large saucepan and stir in vinegar and sugar. Bring to a rolling boil, stirring constantly. Add pectin. Bring to the boil again. Cook, stirring occasionally, for about 30 minutes or until it gives a setting test. Skim if necessary. Pour into hot, clean, dry jars. Seal when cold.
Makes about 6 cups.

BARBECUE SAUCE

The prepared chilli used in this recipe is available in the herb and spice section of the supermarket. The chilli requires no preparation and once opened the jar should be stored in the refrigerator.

2kg ripe tomatoes

2 Granny Smith apples

3 onions

$1/4$ cup soft brown sugar

1 or 2 tablespoons prepared chilli

2 teaspoons dry mustard

1 cup wine vinegar

$1/2$ teaspoon salt

$1/2$ teaspoon freshly ground black pepper

Chop and core the tomatoes. Chop and core the apples. Peel and chop the onions. Mix the tomatoes, apples, onions, sugar, chilli, mustard, vinegar, salt and pepper together in a large saucepan or preserving pan. Bring to the boil and simmer uncovered, stirring occasionally until the mixture is thick. Cool slightly, then blend or process until smooth. Sieve, discarding pulp. Reheat sauce until boiling then pour into hot, clean, dry bottles. Seal when cold.

Makes about 4 cups.

Barbecue Sauce.

TASTE OF SUMMER

SUMMER VEGETABLE AND PASTA BAKE

Eggplant is a magnificent vegetable but if it isn't your thing, try using zucchini in this recipe instead. Any cheese of your choice can be used instead of mozzarella, too.

1 large eggplant
Salt
1 onion
2 cloves garlic
$1/4$ cup extra virgin olive oil
400g can tomatoes in juice
$1/4$ cup tomato paste
1 teaspoon sweet basil leaves
1 teaspoon marjoram leaves
Freshly ground black pepper
300g conchiglie
2 cups grated mozzarella cheese

Trim eggplant and cut into thin slices about $1/2$cm thick. Place in a large sieve or colander and sprinkle over salt, making sure cut surfaces of eggplant are covered lightly with salt. Leave while preparing the rest of the dish. Peel and chop onion finely. Crush, peel and chop garlic. Heat 1 tablespoon of the oil in a saucepan and saute onion and garlic over a low heat for 5 minutes, or until onion is clear. Add tomatoes, tomato paste, basil, marjoram and pepper and cook for 5 minutes. Wash salt from eggplant and wipe slices with paper towels. Heat remaining oil and quickly fry eggplant slices until golden. Oil an ovenproof dish and layer a third of the eggplant, pasta, tomato sauce and cheese. Repeat twice more. Bake at 180°C for 30 minutes, or until cheese is golden.

Serves 4.

Fresh Pumpkin Pickle

Fresh pickles are a delicious accompaniment to a meal. Store in an airtight container in the fridge for a week to ten days. This is absolutely scrumptious.

500g peeled and deseeded pumpkin

2 green chillies

2 red chillies

1/2 cup coconut cream

1/4 cup brown sugar

1 teaspoon salt

4 cloves garlic

1 tablespoon peanut oil

1 teaspoon ground coriander

1/4 cup desiccated coconut

Cut pumpkin into 2 x 5cm sticks. Deseed chillies and cut flesh into thin slices. Mix coconut cream, sugar, salt and green chillies together. Bring to the boil. Add pumpkin and cook for 8 to 10 minutes or until just tender. Cool. Crush and peel garlic and cut into slivers. Heat oil in a frying pan and saute garlic and coriander for 1 minute. Remove from heat and add red chillies and coconut. Mix into pumpkin mixture. Serve warm or cold.

Makes 1 1/2 cups.

Broccoli with Lemon Yoghurt Sauce, European Beans, Fresh Pumpkin Pickle and Designer Beetroot.

Broccoli with Lemon Yoghurt Sauce

500g broccoli

1 onion

2 cloves garlic

1 tablespoon olive oil

1 teaspoon grated lemon rind

2 teaspoons french mustard

3/4 cup natural unsweetened yoghurt

Salt

Freshly ground black pepper

Wash broccoli. Trim and cut in even-sized florets. Steam, boil or microwave until tender. Drain. While broccoli is cooking, peel onion and chop finely. Crush, peel and chop garlic. Heat oil in a saucepan and saute onion and garlic for 5 minutes or until soft but not coloured. Add lemon rind, mustard, yoghurt and salt to onion mixture and bring to the boil. Do not boil. Place broccoli in a serving dish and pour over yoghurt mixture. Grind over black pepper. Serve immediately.

Serves 4.

EUROPEAN BEANS

Beans are difficult to do something interesting with at the best of times. Try this for a new angle.

400g can tomatoes in juice
500g green beans
2 cloves garlic
2 tablespoons oil
1 teaspoon dried basil
Salt
Freshly ground black pepper

Cut tomatoes into large pieces. Wash beans and snap off ends. Crush, peel and chop the garlic. Heat the oil in a large frying pan with a lid. Add the garlic and cook until golden. Add tomatoes and beans and cook for 10 minutes or until beans are tender but firm. Remove beans with a slotted spoon and place on a dish. Bring tomato mixture to the boil and cook until the sauce thickens. Stir in the basil. Return beans to pan and mix to coat. Season with salt and freshly ground black pepper.

Serves 4.

DESIGNER BEETROOT

1kg beetroot
1 red chilli or $^1/_2$ teaspoon dried chilli powder
$1^1/_2$ cups natural unsweetened yoghurt
1 teaspoon ground cumin
1 tablespoon chopped fresh coriander or parsley

Wash beetroot and trim stalk ends. Boil, steam or oven bake until tender. This will take about 30 minutes for boiling, 35 minutes for steaming or about 1 hour if baking wrapped in foil at 180°C. Deseed chilli and cut flesh into thin strips. Mix chilli, yoghurt and cumin together. Peel cooked beetroot. Cut into small cubes and place in a bowl in a pyramid shape or place in individual bowls. Pour over yoghurt mixture and serve immediately, garnished with chopped coriander or parsley.

Serves 6 to 8.

SWEET TREATS

Summer means holidays, entertaining and plenty of outdoor activities that all require the cake tins to be filled with goodies and the cook's head to have a repertoire of simple dessert ideas to call on.

When the weather is hot and life is busy, sweet treats that are quick and easy to prepare are the answer to every cook's prayers.

The recipes that follow meet the demands of summer and give the cook a chance to relax too.

CRUNCHOATLOTS

150g butter

2 tablespoons golden syrup

³/₄ cup soft brown sugar

¹/₂ cup coconut

2 cups rolled oats

¹/₂ cup flour

Melt butter, golden syrup and brown sugar in a saucepan large enough to mix all the ingredients. Mix in coconut, oats and flour until combined. Using a measuring spoon, roll tablespoonsful into balls. Place on a greased oven tray allowing room for spreading. Flatten with a spoon. Bake at 180°C for 10 minutes or until lightly browned. Cool on a cooling rack.

Makes 26.

ALMOND MELTS

150g butter

³/₄ cup sugar

1 teaspoon almond essence

1 ¹/₄ cups flour

1 teaspoon baking powder

¹/₄ cup slivered almonds

Melt butter in a saucepan large enough to mix all the ingredients. Mix in sugar and almond essence. Sift flour and baking powder into saucepan. Using a measuring spoon, measure tablespoonsful of mixture and roll into balls. Place on a greased oven tray. Flatten with the palm of your hand. Press a few almonds onto the surface. Bake at 190°C for 15 minutes or until lightly golden.

Makes about 24.

Crunchoatlots,
Chocolate Biscuits,
Almond Melts and
Speedy Shrewsbury Biscuits

CHOCOLATE BISCUITS

200g butter

1 cup sugar

$^1/_4$ cup cocoa

1 egg

2 cups flour

2 teaspoons baking powder

$^1/_4$ cup chocolate melts

Melt butter with sugar and cocoa in a saucepan large enough to mix all the ingredients. Cool slightly then beat in egg with a wooden spoon until combined. Sift flour and baking powder into the saucepan. Mix until combined. Using a measuring spoon, measure tablespoonsful of mixture and roll into balls. Place on a greased oven tray. Flatten with a fork in a criss-cross pattern. Bake at 180°C for 10 to 15 minutes or until lightly browned. Cool on a cooling rack. Melt chocolate in the microwave or over hot water. Drizzle off the tines of a fork over the biscuits. Leave until chocolate sets.

Makes about 36.

SPEEDY SHREWSBURY BISCUITS

When travelling I always find myself in the kitchenware shops. I found the cutter used for these biscuits in Munich. There are many things in the kitchen that can be used to cut the same effect.

400g packet sweet short pastry

Raspberry jam

Icing sugar

Roll the pastry out on a lightly floured board. Using a 6cm biscuit cutter, cut pastry into rounds. Using an *hors-d'oeuvre* cutter, the end of a piping nozzle or something else with a small hole that can be used for cutting, cut one or more holes in half the biscuits. Place rounds on a floured oven tray. Bake at 190°C for 10 minutes or until lightly golden. Cool on a cooling rack. Spread the biscuits without the hole with jam almost to the edges. Top with holed biscuits. Dust with sifted icing sugar.

Makes 16.

AMERICAN BROWNIE

This rich and yummy recipe has always been a great success for anyone I have given it to.

250g butter
$^1/_2$ cup cocoa
$1^1/_2$ cups sugar
4 eggs
1 cup flour
1 teaspoon baking powder
1 teaspoon vanilla essence

Melt butter in a saucepan large enough to mix all the ingredients. Mix in cocoa. Remove from heat and stir in sugar. Add eggs and beat well using a wooden spoon. Sift flour and baking powder into the mixture. Add vanilla essence and mix to combine. Pour into a greased 20 x 30cm sponge roll tin. Bake at 180°C for 25 to 30 minutes or until brownie springs back when lightly touched. Cut into bars while still warm. Ice with chocolate icing if wished.

MUESLI SLICE

125g butter
$^3/_4$ cup soft brown sugar
2 tablespoons golden syrup
$1^1/_4$ cups toasted muesli
$^3/_4$ cup raisins
1 cup wholemeal flour
$1^1/_2$ teaspoons baking powder
$^1/_2$ teaspoon mixed spice
Lemon icing

Melt butter, brown sugar and golden syrup in a saucepan large enough to mix all the ingredients. Add muesli and raisins. Sift in flour, baking powder and mixed spice, returning husks left in sifter to the saucepan. Mix until combined. Press mixture into an 18 x 28cm slice tin. Bake at 180°C for 15 to 20 minutes. When cool, ice with lemon icing and cut into squares.

American Brownie & Muesli Slice

TASTE OF SUMMER

Italian Biscotti

Add ¹/₂ cup shelled pistachio nuts to this recipe if you wish.

1 x 70g packet blanched almonds

¹/₂ cup shelled pistachio nuts

2 cups flour

1 teaspoon baking powder

Pinch salt

¹/₂ cup caster sugar

1 teaspoon vanilla essence

2 eggs

1 egg white

Toast almonds at 180°C for 5 to 10 minutes or until pale golden. Allow to cool then chop roughly. Sift flour, baking powder and salt into a mixing bowl. Add caster sugar and stir until combined. Lightly beat vanilla essence and eggs together then add to dry ingredients. Mix until well combined. Turn on to a lightly floured surface and work in the nuts. Add more flour if necessary until a firm dough is reached. Divide mixture in half and shape into logs about 5cm wide. Place on a greased oven tray. Lightly beat egg white then brush each log with egg white. Bake at 180°C for 35 minutes or until cooked through. Allow to cool slightly then cut each log on the diagonal into 1cm wide slices. Place slices on an oven tray. Reduce temperature to 150°C and bake for a further 10 minutes or until dry.

Makes about 40.

SIENA CAKE

125g blanched almonds

125g hazelnuts

$^{1}/_{2}$ cup mixed peel

75g cooking chocolate

$^{3}/_{4}$ cup flour

2 tablespoons cocoa

1 teaspoon ground cinnamon

$^{1}/_{4}$ cup sugar

$^{1}/_{2}$ cup honey

$^{1}/_{4}$ cup water

Icing sugar

Roughly chop the almonds. Roast in a shallow baking tray at 160°C for 10 minutes or until lightly coloured. Roast hazelnuts at 160°C for 15-18 minutes or until skins begin to darken. Rub to loosen skins. Remove skins and chop nuts. Finely chop mixed peel. Roughly chop chocolate. Sift flour, cocoa and cinnamon into a bowl. Mix in nuts, chocolate and peel. Put sugar, honey and water in a saucepan. Stir over low heat until sugar dissolves. Increase heat and bring the mixture to the boil, stirring constantly. Boil without stirring until the soft ball stage. This is when a drop of mixture forms a soft ball in cold water. Mix the sugar mixture and chocolate into the flour and nut mixture until combined. Working quickly, spread into a baking paper lined 20cm sponge sandwich tin. Smooth the top with the back of a wet spoon. Bake at 160°C for 35 to 40 minutes. Cool in the tin. Dust with icing sugar and serve cut into thin wedges.

Italian Biscotti (left) & Siena Cake

LEMON CURD CAKE

This makes a great dessert cake. Lemon curd can be bought readymade or you can make your own. It's also called lemon butter or lemon cheese. This is a fairly dense moist cake with a magnificent flavour.

1¹/₂ cups flour

3 teaspoons baking powder

¹/₂ cup custard powder

1 cup sugar

¹/₂ cup lemon curd

³/₄ cup milk

3 eggs

150g soft butter

Icing sugar

LEMON CURD SAUCE

¹/₄ cup lemon curd

¹/₂ cup natural unsweetened yoghurt

¹/₂ cup whipped cream

Sift flour, baking powder and custard powder into a mixer bowl. Add sugar, lemon curd, milk, eggs and butter. Beat on medium speed for 7 minutes. Pour into a baking paper-lined 20cm cake tin. Bake at 180°C for 50 to 60 minutes or until cake springs back when lightly touched. Serve dusted with sifted icing sugar and lemon curd sauce.

LEMON CURD SAUCE

Mix lemon curd, yoghurt and cream together.

From back, clockwise: Lemon Curd Cake, Lemon Torte and Madeira Cake

LEMON TORTE

This is one of those special cakes with no flour that can be quickly rustled up for an afternoon tea or dessert. Lemon curd is also called lemon honey or lemon cheese. It can be bought readymade from the jam section in the supermarket. You can double this recipe and fill the cake with lemon cream if wished.

3 eggs

¹/₂ cup caster sugar

1 tablespoon grated lemon rind

3 tablespoons lemon juice

¹/₂ cup semolina

Icing sugar

¹/₂ cup cream

2 tablespoons lemon curd

Separate the eggs. Beat the egg yolks and sugar with an electric mixer until pale and thick. On a slow speed beat in the lemon rind, juice and semolina until combined. Beat egg whites until stiff and fold into egg yolk mixture using a low mixer speed, or fold in by hand. Pour into a baking paper-lined 20cm round sponge sandwich tin, or two tins if you have doubled the recipe. Bake at 180°C for 30 to 40 minutes or until cake springs back when lightly touched. Leave in tin for 10 minutes before turning onto a cooling rack. Remove paper while still warm. Dust cake with sifted icing sugar. Whip cream until soft and fold in lemon curd. Serve with the cake.

MADEIRA CAKE

125g soft butter

¹/₂ cup sugar

1 teaspoon vanilla essence

2 eggs

1¹/₂ cups flour

3 teaspoons baking powder

¹/₂ cup milk

Place butter, sugar, vanilla essence, eggs, flour, baking powder and milk in a mixer bowl. Beat on low speed until just combined. Increase speed and beat for 2 minutes. Pour into a baking paper-lined 22cm loaf tin and bake at 180°C for 50 to 60 minutes or until cake springs back when lightly touched. Leave in tin for 10 minutes before turning out onto a cooling rack. Ice if wished.

TASTE OF SUMMER

CHOCOLATE CHERRY FOREST CAKE

Dust this cake with sifted icing sugar or ice with chocolate icing as an alternative to the jam and flake bars.

150g butter

1 cup chocolate melts

1 cup sugar

$^1/_4$ cup cocoa

3 eggs

1 teaspoon vanilla essence

2 cups flour

2 teaspoons baking powder

1 teaspoon baking soda

1 cup low fat milk

$^3/_4$ cup halved glace cherries

1 tablespoon jam

2 chocolate flake bars

Place butter, chocolate melts, sugar and cocoa in a saucepan large enough to mix all the ingredients. Heat until butter and chocolate melt. Cool slightly. Beat in eggs with a wooden spoon. Add vanilla essence, sifted flour, baking powder, baking soda and milk. Beat until smooth. Pour mixture into a baking paper-lined 20cm round cake tin. Dry cherries on a paper towel and sprinkle over mixture in cake tin. Bake at 180°C for 1$^1/_4$ hours or until cake springs back when lightly touched. Leave in the tin to cool for 10 minutes before turning onto a cooling rack. Brush top of cake with jam while still warm. When cold, decorate with broken flake bars.

WHOLEMEAL CHOCOLATE CAKE

Using wholemeal flour in your baking adds fibre and gives baked goodies a more grainy texture. This is a good everyday chocolate cake. Corn, safflower, grapeseed or any other oil that is not strongly flavoured is suitable for this cake.

1 cup wholemeal flour

1 cup flour

1/4 cup cocoa

1 teaspoon cinnamon

2 teaspoons baking powder

1 teaspoon baking soda

1 cup soft brown sugar

2 eggs

3/4 cup oil

3/4 cup water

Mix flours, cocoa, cinnamon, baking powder, baking soda and brown sugar together in a bowl until blended. Make a well in the dry ingredients. Beat eggs, oil and water together in a bowl. Pour into well and mix with a wooden spoon until smooth. Pour into a baking paper-lined 20cm plain or moulded ring tin. Bake at 180°C for 35 to 45 minutes or until cake springs back when lightly touched. Leave in tin for 10 minutes before turning onto a cooling rack.

CHOCOLATE MARBLE CAKE

This cake looks stunning if made in a moulded ring tin.

125g butter

3/4 cup sugar

3 eggs

1/2 cup milk

1 1/2 cups flour

3 teaspoons baking powder

2 teaspoons vanilla essence

2 tablespoons cocoa

2 tablespoons boiling water

1/4 cup dark chocolate melts

1/4 cup white chocolate melts

Melt butter in a mixer bowl in the microwave or over hot water. Add sugar, eggs, milk, flour, baking powder and vanilla essence to butter. Mix on low speed until combined. Increase speed to medium and beat for 3 minutes or until smooth. Pour half the mixture into a well greased 20cm moulded ring tin. Mix cocoa and water together and mix into remaining half of cake mixture. Pour over plain mixture. Using a fork, squiggle the tines gently through both mixtures to marble. Bake at 160°C for 55 to 60 minutes or until cake springs back when lightly touched. Leave in tin for 10 minutes before turning onto a cooling rack. Melt chocolate melts separately. Drizzle chocolates over cake when cold.

*From left, clockwise:
Chocolate Marble Cake,
Wholemeal Chocolate Cake and
Chocolate Cherry Forest Cake*

BUTTONS

They are delicious at any time of the year.

150g butter

5 tablespoons sugar

$^1/_4$ teaspoon vanilla essence

$1^1/_4$ cups flour

6 tablespoons cornflour

$^1/_2$ cup finely chopped pecans or walnuts

About 2 tablespoons jam

Melt butter in a saucepan large enough to mix all the ingredients. Remove from heat. Stir in sugar and vanilla essence. Sift flour and cornflour into the saucepan. Mix until well combined. Roll tablespoonsful of mixture into balls. Roll in nuts and place on a greased oven tray. Make an indentation in the centre of each biscuit. Spoon a little jam in the centre. Bake at 160°C for 15 to 20 minutes or until pale brown.

Makes 24

Buttons

ITALIAN FIG CAKE

2 eggs

³/₄ cup sugar

1 cup flour

1 ¹/₂ teaspoons baking powder

¹/₄ cup milk

1 tablespooon toasted breadcrumbs

Icing sugar

FILLING

1 ¹/₂ cups chopped dried figs

³/₄ cup finely chopped walnuts

¹/₄ cup marmalade

2 teaspoons grated orange rind

¹/₈ teaspoon ground cloves

¹/₂ teaspoon ground cinnamon

Beat eggs and sugar together until light and thick. Sift flour and baking powder and fold in alternately with milk into the cake batter. Grease and baking paper line a 20cm cake tin. Sprinkle with the breadcrumbs. Spoon half the cake batter into the cake tin. Carefully dot fig filling over the top and spread over the cake batter. Pour remaining batter over the top. Bake at 180°C for 35 to 40 minutes or until an inserted skewer comes out clean. Dust with icing sugar. Serve warm as a dessert cake or cold with tea or coffee.

FILLING

Mix all ingredients together.

Serves 6.

Italian Fig Cake

TASTE OF SUMMER

FRUIT CAKE

Use as one large cake or cut into four for small cakes. Use high grade flour or flour suitable for making fruit cakes.

1kg mixed dried fruit
1 cup flour
400g butter
3 cups soft brown sugar
5 eggs
1 tablespoon grated orange rind
1 tablespoon grated lemon rind
2¹/₂ cups flour
3 teaspoons mixed spice
2 teaspoons ground cinnamon
¹/₂ teaspoon baking soda
¹/₄ cup cold tea

Line the bottom of a 28 x 36cm roasting dish with a layer of baking paper. Layer 4 to 6 layers of brown paper or newspaper for the tin to sit on in the oven. In a large plastic bag mix dried fruit with first measure of flour. Melt butter and brown sugar together in a saucepan large enough to mix all the ingredients. Cool slightly, then beat in eggs with a wooden spoon. Add orange and lemon rinds and sift second measure of flour, mixed spice, cinnamon and baking soda into saucepan and add cold tea. Mix until combined. Spread mixture evenly into the prepared tin. Sit tin on paper in oven and bake at 150°C for 1¹/₂ hours, or until an inserted skewer comes out clean. Leave cake to cool in tin. Trim edges and cut into four cakes.

Fruit Cake

TUI'S RICH FRUIT CAKE

If you like a moist fruit cake you will enjoy the flavour and texture of this one.

$2^1/_2$ cups raisins

$1^1/_2$ cups sultanas

$^1/_2$ cup glace cherries

$^1/_2$ cup chopped mixed peel

$^1/_2$ cup flour

250g butter

$1^1/_2$ cups soft brown sugar

2 tablespoons treacle

4 eggs

2 teaspoons grated orange rind

2 teaspoons grated lemon rind

1 teaspoon vanilla essence

$1^3/_4$ cups flour

$^1/_2$ teaspoon mixed spice

$^1/_2$ teaspoon ground cinnamon

$^1/_4$ teaspoon ground nutmeg

$^1/_4$ teaspoon ground ginger

$^1/_4$ teaspoon baking soda

2 to 3 tablespoons brandy

Line the sides and bottom of a 23cm round cake tin with 3 layers of newspaper, 1 layer of brown paper and 1 layer of baking paper. Mix raisins, sultanas, cherries and mixed peel together. Mix through first measure of flour. Melt butter, brown sugar and treacle together in a saucepan large enough to mix all the ingredients. Remove from heat and cool. Add eggs and beat well with a wooden spoon. Mix in oranges and lemon rinds and vanilla essence. Sift flour, mixed spice, cinnamon, nutmeg, ginger and baking soda into the saucepan and mix until combined. Spoon into the prepared tin. Smooth the surface and sprinkle lightly with water. This keeps the top level. Bake at 150°C for $1^1/_2$ hours. Lower temperature to 130°C and cook for a further 2 to $2^1/_2$ hours or until a skewer comes out clean when tested. Allow cake to cool in tin. Pour brandy over the cake.

SIMPLE SUMMER BERRY SALAD

Any combination of berries will do for this simple salad idea.

2 cups strawberries
2 tablespoons sugar
2 cups raspberries
2 cups boysenberries
Icing sugar
CUSTARD CREAM
1 cup cream
1 cup readymade custard

Hull strawberries. Cut in half and sprinkle over sugar. Set aside for 1 hour. Clean raspberries and boysenberries and mix with strawberries. Pile berry mixture into the centre of 6 plates. Dust with icing sugar and serve with custard cream and sponge fingers.

CUSTARD CREAM

Whip cream until soft. Fold custard into cream.

Serves 6.

FRESH FRUIT SALAD

Soft berry fruits are best left out of this sort of fruit salad, or add them just before serving.

4 cups mixed fresh seasonal fruits such as apples, cherries, strawberries, kiwifruit, nectarines, peaches
$^{1}/_{2}$ cup orange and mango juice
2 tablespoons sugar
$^{1}/_{4}$ cup passionfruit pulp

Prepare fruits, chopping to give a variety of shapes. Cubes, slices and circles of fruit add interest to a fruit salad. Heat juice and sugar together until reduced by a third. Cool. Pour over fruit with passionfruit pulp. Serve lightly chilled.

Serves 4.

Simple Summer Berry Salad and Fresh Fruit Salad

CATHEDRAL WINDOW CAKES

These cakes make a great Christmas gift. They are not cheap to make but could solve a gift problem. Measure loaf tins from the top edges and use high grade flour or flour suitable for fruit cakes.

1kg mixed glace fruits such as pears, pineapple, cherries, apricots
350g blanched almonds
650g brazil nuts
9 eggs
1¹/₂ cups caster sugar
3 teaspoons vanilla essence
¹/₂ cup brandy
2¹/₄ cups flour
2 teaspoons baking powder
2 teaspoons mixed spice

Chop the glace fruits if large. Mix fruit, almonds and brazil nuts together. In a large bowl beat eggs, caster sugar, vanilla essence and brandy together. Fold sifted flour, baking powder and mixed spice into egg mixture. Mix fruit and nuts into egg mixture until combined. Divide mixture evenly between four baking paper-lined 20 x 10cm loaf tins. Bake at 160°C for 1¹/₂ hours or until an inserted skewer comes out clean. Cool in tins. Remove lining paper and wrap in foil or seal in a plastic bag until ready to wrap for giving.

Makes 4 loaf-shaped cakes.

Fruit Fingers, "Oh Crumbs" Biscuits and Cathedral Window Cakes

FRUIT FINGERS

4¹/₂ cups mixed fruit such as dates, raisins, sultanas
³/₄ cup soft brown sugar
50g butter
2 teaspoons mixed spice
1 cup orange juice
2 cups soft breadcrumbs
2 x 350g rolls pre-rolled flaky pastry
2 tablespoons caster sugar

Place the mixed fruit, brown sugar, butter, mixed spice and orange juice in a saucepan. Bring to the boil, stirring until butter melts. Cover and remove from heat. Set aside to cool. Mix breadcrumbs into fruit mixture. Unroll one packet of pastry onto a lightly floured oven tray. Spread fruit mixture over pastry to within 1cm of the edge. Dampen edges with water. Unroll second packet of pastry over the top of the fruit filling. Press edges together. Prick top pastry with a fork. Sprinkle sugar over. Bake at 210°C for 15 to 20 minutes or until pastry is golden. When cold, cut into fingers.

"OH CRUMBS" BISCUITS

Top these biscuits with a walnut if you feel generous.

200g soft butter
1¹/₂ cups sugar
2 tablespoons golden syrup
2 teaspoons vanilla essence
2 eggs
1¹/₄ cups flour
2 cups coconut
1¹/₂ cups toasted breadcrumbs
2 teaspoons baking powder

Place butter, sugar, golden syrup, vanilla essence and eggs in a mixer bowl. Mix to combine. Add flour, coconut, breadcrumbs and baking powder to the bowl and mix on low speed until combined. Roll tablespoonsful into balls. Place on a greased oven tray. Flatten with a fork. Bake at 180°C for 10 to 15 minutes or until golden.

Makes about 70.

KANSAS PECAN PIE

2 eggs

1 cup brown sugar

84g packet vanilla instant pudding

1 cup evaporated milk

1 cup chopped pecans

400g packet sweet short pastry

1 cup pecan halves

Lightly beat eggs, brown sugar and instant pudding together. Mix in evaporated milk and chopped pecans. Roll out pastry on a lightly floured board. Line a 22cm flan dish with pastry. Trim to fit. Pour in filling. Arrange pecan halves over surface. Bake at 200ºC for 10 minutes then reduce heat to 160ºC and bake for a further 30 minutes or until golden and set.

Serves 6.

QUICK FRUIT TART

Use a variety of fruits for this flan to give plenty of colour contrast.

400g packet sweet short pastry

2 x 150g pots vanilla or banana dairy food

2 to 3 cups fresh or drained canned fruit

¹/₂ cup apricot jam

Roll pastry out on a lightly floured board. Use to line a 24cm flan dish or three small 12cm flan dishes. Bake blind at 190ºC for 10 minutes. Remove baking blind material and cook for a further 5 minutes to dry out. Cool. Spread dairy food over base of pastry. Prepare fruit as necessary. Arrange fruit over dairy food. Warm apricot jam and brush liberally over fruit. Chill before serving.

Serves 6.

Custard Tart (top left), Quick Fruit Tarts, Mince Pies and Kansas Pecan Pie

CUSTARD TART

Extra egg yolks can be used in this tart and cream can be substituted for milk for an especially fatty treat.

400g packet sweet short pastry

4 eggs

¹/₄ cup sugar

2 teaspoons vanilla essence

1 tablespoon cornflour

1¹/₄ cups milk

Ground nutmeg

Roll pastry out on a lightly floured board. Line a 20cm pie or flan dish with the pastry. Bake blind at 200°C for 10 to 15 minutes or until starting to colour. Remove baking blind material. Return to oven for 2 to 3 minutes to dry out. Beat eggs and sugar until combined. Try not to let eggs become frothy. Mix in vanilla essence. Mix cornflour with a little of the measured milk. Mix into the eggs with remaining milk. Pour into pastry shell through a sieve. Sprinkle with ground nutmeg. Bake at 200°C for 5 minutes. Reduce heat to 160°C for 30 to 35 minutes or until set.

Serves 6.

MINCE PIES

400g packet sweet short pastry

1¹/₄ cups Christmas mincemeat

Icing sugar

Roll pastry out on a lightly floured board to 2mm thickness. Cut out 7¹/₂cm rounds and use to line patty pans. Three-quarter fill pastry cases with Christmas mincemeat. Re-roll pastry and cut out 7cm lids. Using a cardboard template or cocktail cutter, cut out shapes from centre of pastry tops. Place tops on pies and press to seal. Cut-outs can be used instead of full lids. Bake at 190°C for 15 to 20 minutes or until lightly golden. Serve warm sprinkled with icing sugar.

Makes 14.

TASTE OF SUMMER

TIRAMISU

5 tablespoons custard powder

3 cups milk

3 tablespoons sugar

1 egg white

$^1/_2$ cup brandy

125g packet sponge fingers

250g pot cream cheese

$^1/_4$ cup strong black coffee

300mls cream

Mix custard powder with quarter cup of the measured milk. Heat remaining milk. Pour heated milk onto custard powder mixture. Return to saucepan. Stir in sugar. Cook over medium heat, stirring constantly until mixture boils and thickens. Remove from heat. Allow to cool. Beat egg white until stiff but not dry. Fold into custard. Stir in two tablespoons of the measured brandy. Dip sponge fingers in remaining brandy and arrange on the bottom of a serving dish. Combine cream cheese and coffee, beating until smooth. Spread one-third of the coffee mixture over the sponge fingers. Spoon one-third of the custard mixture over. Repeat until all the ingredients are used. Refrigerate until cold. Whip cream until thick. Pipe cream on top of custard.

Serves 8 to 10.

CASSATA

No Italian-style cookbook would be complete without the inclusion of this popular dessert. Traditionally, cassata was made with ricotta cheese to which was added a variety of dried fruit and nuts. This mixture is used to fill a sponge-lined mould then chilled. I have chosen the more "popular" interpretation of this dessert, the icecream version.

1 litre vanilla icecream

$^1/_4$ to $^1/_2$ teaspoon almond essence

300ml cream

2 tablespoons sugar

$^1/_2$ cup toasted almonds

50g dark chocolate

$^1/_2$ cup chopped glace fruit

Soften the icecream. Mix in the almond essence and use to line the base and sides of a 1 litre pudding basin leaving a cavity in the middle for the fruit mixture. A metal basin is good for this recipe. Freeze until firm. Whip the cream and sugar together until peaks form. Chop the almonds and chocolate. Fold the glace fruit, almonds and chocolate into the whipped cream. Use to fill the cavity of the icecream. Cover with foil and freeze until firm.

When ready to serve, dip the basin into hot water very quickly two or three times then invert and shake sharply onto a serving plate. To serve, cut into wedges.

Serves 6

Tiramisu & Cassata (bottom)

GATEAU PITHIVIERS

This is a traditional French cake eaten on New Year's Eve. Whoever gets the coin from the Pithivier is King or Queen for the night.

100g butter
1/2 cup sugar
2 eggs
1/2 cup flour
2 x 70g packets ground almonds
1/2 teaspoon almond essence
2 sheets flaky puff pastry
1/4 cup apricot jam
1 egg yolk
1 tablespoon water
Icing sugar

Melt butter and sugar in a saucepan. Beat in eggs. Mix in flour, almonds and almond essence. Mix lightly until combined. Cut a 24cm round from one pastry sheet. Spread pastry round with jam, leaving a 2cm border. Spread almond mixture over jam. Place a real silver coin into the filling or wrap any other type of coin in foil and place in filling. Brush edges of pastry with water. Cut a 24cm diameter circle from the second pastry sheet. Place over almond mixture. Press edges together. Cut 10 curved cuts from the centre of the pithivier to 1 1/2cm from the outside edge of the pastry top. Beat egg yolk and water together and brush over top surface of pastry. Bake at 220°C for 25 minutes or until golden. Dust with icing sugar while hot. Leave to cool before cutting.

Serves 8.

QUICK LEMON MERINGUE PIE

You must use the right lemon variety for this recipe. Use lemon with a light coloured skin and light flesh

400g packet sweet short pastry
FILLING
4 egg yolks
397g can sweetened condensed milk
1/2 cup lemon juice
1 tablespoon grated lemon rind
1 egg white
TOPPING
3 egg whites
1/2 cup sugar

Roll out pastry on a lightly floured board to 2mm thickness. Use to line the base and sides of a 22cm flan dish. Bake blind at 200°C for 10 minutes. Remove baking blind material and cook for a further 2 minutes to dry out. Cool while making filling. Pour filling into pastry shell. Spread meringue over filling. Bake at 180°C for 8 to 10 minutes or until golden.

FILLING

Mix egg yolks, condensed milk, lemon juice and lemon rind together. Beat egg white until soft peaks form and fold into lemon mixture.

TOPPING

Beat egg whites until soft peaks form. Beat in sugar, a little at a time. Continue beating until thick and glossy.

Serves 6 to 8.

Quick Lemon Meringue Pie and Gateau Pithiviers

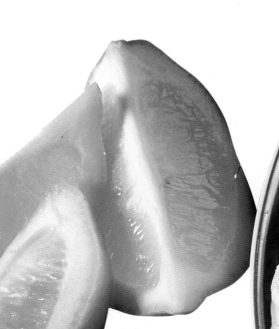

INDEX